Xamarin Continuous Integration and Delivery

Team Services, Test Cloud, and HockeyApp

Gerald Versluis

Foreword by Donovan Brown

Apress®

Xamarin Continuous Integration and Delivery: Team Services, Test Cloud, and HockeyApp

Gerald Versluis
Sittard, The Netherlands

ISBN-13 (pbk): 978-1-4842-2715-2   ISBN-13 (electronic): 978-1-4842-2716-9
DOI 10.1007/978-1-4842-2716-9

Library of Congress Control Number: 2017941246

Managing Director: Welmoed Spahr
Editorial Director: Todd Green
Acquisitions Editor: Jonathan Gennick
Development Editor: Laura Berendson
Technical Reviewer: Adam Pedley
Coordinating Editor: Jill Balzano
Copy Editor: Kim Wimpsett
Compositor: SPi Global
Indexer: SPi Global
Artist: SPi Global

Distributed to the book trade worldwide by Springer Science+Business Media New York, 233 Spring Street, 6th Floor, New York, NY 10013. Phone 1-800-SPRINGER, fax (201) 348-4505, e-mail orders-ny@springer-sbm.com, or visit www.springeronline.com. Apress Media, LLC is a California LLC and the sole member (owner) is Springer Science + Business Media Finance Inc (SSBM Finance Inc). SSBM Finance Inc is a Delaware corporation.

For information on translations, please e-mail rights@apress.com, or visit www.apress.com/rights-permissions.

Apress titles may be purchased in bulk for academic, corporate, or promotional use. eBook versions and licenses are also available for most titles. For more information, reference our Print and eBook Bulk Sales web page at www.apress.com/bulk-sales.

Any source code or other supplementary material referenced by the author in this book is available to readers on GitHub via the book's product page, located at www.apress.com/9781484227152. For more detailed information, please visit www.apress.com/source-code.

Printed on acid-free paper

Contents at a Glance

Contents

Foreword

As a principal DevOps program manager for Microsoft, I was given the opportunity to define *DevOps*. After a month of soul searching, I came up with this single cohesive definition: DevOps is the union of people, process, and products to enable continuous delivery of value to our end users. This is true for all types of development, including mobile. Visual Studio Team Services (VSTS) is the product from Microsoft that enables DevOps for any language targeting any platform. With the help of this book, you are taken from creating your VSTS account all the way to deploying your application. The author gives a quick tour of all the functionality provided by VSTS and then jumps right in to helping with your first build.

Gerald Versluis touches on all three *P*'s of DevOps: people, process, and products. Most of the book covers the products—specifically VSTS—but also discusses other products, including HockeyApp, Xamarin Test Cloud, and Microsoft partner products. Throughout the book, Gerald explains the process that guides teams on their DevOps journey. Additionally, he discusses how to address the toughest *P*: people.

DevOps has benefits for projects of all sizes. Gerald does a great job of not just telling you how DevOps can benefit you and your organization but also explaining why these practices are so important. I always describe VSTS as everything you need to turn an idea into a working piece of software, and *Xamarin Continuous Integration and Delivery* proves that for mobile.

—Donovan Brown
Principal DevOps Program Manager
Microsoft

About the Author

Gerald Versluis is a full-stack software developer and Microsoft MVP from Holland. After years of experience working with Xamarin and .NET technologies, he has been involved in numerous projects, in all kinds of roles. A great number of these projects are Xamarin apps.

Not only does he like to code, but he is keen on spreading his knowledge, as well as gaining some in the bargain. Gerald involves himself in speaking, providing training sessions, and writing blogs (https://blog.verslu.is) and articles in his spare time. You can find him on Twitter with the handle @jfversluis and can find more information on his web site at https://gerald.verslu.is.

About the Technical Reviewer

Adam Pedley is a Microsoft MVP and actively engaged in the Xamarin community. He speaks at technical events and is a contributor and author to several open source projects, including Xamarin Forms. He currently runs the largest community blog dedicated to Xamarin and helps thousands of Xamarin developers around the world, through several online channels.

As a 15-year .NET developer and architect, he has helped government, large businesses, and startups with all aspects of development. Adam is a Xamarin Certified developer and has a bachelor's degree in computer science from Edith Cowan University.

You can read Adam's blog at www.xamarinhelp.com and follow him on Twitter @adpedley.

Acknowledgments

There are a few people I would like to thank for making this all possible.

First, thank you to the people at Apress, especially Jonathan and Jill who have been guiding me through the adventure of writing my first book. Without them it wouldn't look as good as it does now.

I would also like to thank Erwin, Patrick, Steven, and Ben, colleagues and friends. Each of them has helped me with early feedback and has been an inspiration at several stages while writing.

The technical review was in the hands of the skillful Adam Pedley, my friend from afar. Thank you for being willing to proofread my ramblings and ensure everything looks OK.

Despite his busy schedule, Donovan Brown of Microsoft found some spare time to not only proofread my book and provide some invaluable feedback but also write a foreword for it. Thank you for that.

Finally, I would like to thank Laurie for being patient with me and supporting me in whatever dream I am pursuing this time.

Although I did my best to name everyone who has helped me or has otherwise been of any importance to me during this process, I might have forgotten to mention you. For that I am sorry, but I want to thank you nevertheless.

Introduction

Continuous integration and delivery is a concept that we cannot do without anymore. In a world where good software is being delivered at a very high pace, it becomes more and more important to keep up. If you do not, others will steal away your users. Several books already describe this subject, but none of them focuses on Xamarin apps.

As a developer who loves Xamarin, I wanted to fill this gap. I have set up numerous CI/CD pipelines, and it never gets boring. The challenge is always different because no two apps are the same. Also, continuous integration and delivery for an app is different from "normal" applications. You must code sign your applications, abide by the rules for each app store, and let them go through a review process, to say the least. It requires some specific knowledge on how to achieve this in the first place and second on how to weave the steps into an automated pipeline.

With this book, I have created a hands-on guide for setting up a professional, automated building pipeline for yourself. I have focused on Microsoft technologies such as Visual Studio Team Services, HockeyApp, and of course Xamarin. Not only have I tried to describe the concepts behind these tools, but I take you through the actual steps to get things done. By following along from start to finish, you should be able to configure a pipeline for yourself.

To enable you to get the most out of this book, I also cover testing and specifically automated UI tests with Xamarin Test Cloud.

I hope you will enjoy reading my first book as much as I enjoyed writing it. Happy reading and learning!

CHAPTER 1

■ ■ ■

Why an Automated Pipeline?

An *automated pipeline, continuous integration* (CI), and *continuous delivery* (CD) are all
terms that describe the process and tools that help you compile and deliver your software
in an automated way. Since the software publication process remains largely the same,
you do not have to repeat it manually every single time you want to push out a new
version. Repetition is something people are not really good at, but computers are well
suited for doing the same thing over and over again.

In this chapter, you will learn about the high-level terms that will be used in this
book. Moreover, the chapter will explain why it is a good idea to set up a development
pipeline of your own.

While the concept of an automated pipeline is far from new, it does have some
interesting challenges when it is combined with the new world of mobile apps. The
ecosystem of the different app stores differs from "traditional" desktop and web
applications in terms of the freedom you have as a developer to control the environment
on which your app will land. Also, it requires some specific handling to create a package
that is accepted by the different app store vendors. These are all topics that we will look at
throughout the course of this book.

What Is Continuous Integration?

"It works on my machine" is a phrase you will hear a lot when working in software
development.

You can get away with that while working alone, when you are responsible for every
single piece of code in your app. But when you start working in a team or have to set up
a new development environment, there is a chance that you will forget to check in a file,
reference a library from somewhere on your hard drive, and so on. These examples would
all be causes for your app not being able to build anywhere besides within your specific
development environment.

In addition, like every developer, you integrate your full code each time, including
the unit tests for your app. Every time before you check in a new piece of code, you run it
to see whether everything still lights up green, review the code coverage stats, and write
new tests as you go. (You do that, right?) How awesome would it be if all of that testing
work could be done for you automatically? You do not have to memorize a list of things
you have to do or must not do before you are about to check in. Instead, you just get a
signal when something is going wrong.

© Gerald Versluis 2017
G. Versluis, *Xamarin Continuous Integration and Delivery*,
DOI 10.1007/978-1-4842-2716-9_1

Finally, one of the things each developer learns over time is that no matter how good you are, you still have bad days and make mistakes like a real person. There really is just one thing you can do about that, and that is to get some feedback about the mistakes as early on as possible so you can fix them before anyone notices.

Well, continuous integration can help you with all three of these situations. CI encompasses a great number of possibilities to ensure the quality of your app. Basically, it does what it says: CI integrates your code continuously with the rest of the code already there, whether that code has been enriched by other members of your team or is just code that you checked in earlier.

With CI, a version of your app will be created with all the latest sources available at that time, and while doing so, the process will let you know if it still compiles.

From there you can start expanding your build process by letting your unit tests run, sending your app through automated UI tests, loading tests, copying a file to another location, transforming your configuration files, generating a build number, and doing anything else you can think of. The rule of thumb is that anything you can run from a command line can be integrated in your builds.

One of the best and most complete solutions to support you with CI and CD (along with many more features) is Visual Studio Team Services (VSTS) by Microsoft. If you have ever worked with Team Foundation Server (TFS) as a source control tool, you should feel right at home.

VSTS is available online, hosted in an Azure variant of TFS, and actually gets new features before the on-premise TFS does. In addition, it is free (to some extent, of course!).

Besides acting as a source control solution, VSTS has a lot of possibilities. One is the automatic building of your source code, which is one of the aspects this book will be focusing on. Besides that, you can manage your work with Scrum or Kanban boards, edit your code from the web portal, work with branches, search code, push NuGet packages, and do much, much more.

While VSTS is a complete environment and leaves you with little to wish for, there are other good services out there like Bitrise and Fastlane. The focus of this book will be on Microsoft products and thus VSTS, but the appendix includes some pointers to alternative tools that are worth checking out.

What Is Continuous Delivery?

Imagine you are in the middle of coding the next functionality in your software or maybe starting a whole new project altogether and suddenly the tester on your team pops up at your desk with a possible bug in your app. Or, just when some big new functionality is only halfway done, your manager finds you and requests the latest version to show to the client's chief executive officer (CEO). While this is something you want to do, you cannot deliver a stable version without rolling back hours of work, and even then you are hoping that you did not forget anything.

These are just two examples in which continuous delivery can prove to be very useful.

As a logical extension of the continuous integration pipeline, CD takes the bits that have been generated while building (also known as *artifacts*) and delivers them to a certain audience of your choosing. This audience can be a tester on your team, a group of predetermined beta testers, or maybe your girlfriend, but it can also be no one. The fact that you *can* deliver continuously does not mean you *have* to. The fact that delivering to specific environments works is a quality check in itself.

The environments can be the different channels with which you supply your shippable app to end users. Which channel you want to use depends on the requirements you have and the end users you are targeting.

In Chapter 7 you will look at HockeyApp, which is great for distributing your apps in a unified way for all platforms to your end users. It also helps you to collect user feedback, and it has a great software development kit (SDK), which allows you to retrieve detailed crash reports remotely, even for desktop apps.

HockeyApp is an essential tool for the modern developer to detect bugs almost before the user does. However, it cannot be used as a production environment in the case of apps because of the different vendors; Apple, Google, and Microsoft require you to distribute your app though their channels.

The different app stores do have some functionality that allows you to send out test versions. However, the features they offer vary, and more importantly, you, as the developer, need to go through three kinds of app store hoops to get what you want.

As mentioned earlier, there will be a point that you cannot get around the app stores anymore as you will have to distribute your production version through them. However, this does not mean you cannot provide these app stores with your app in an automated way.

Why Do You Need an Automated Build Pipeline?

A "fully featured build pipeline" sounds like something that only big companies can take advantage of, or can even afford. While this may have been true at one point, it sure is not true these days.

So, whether you are a sole developer working on your million-dollar idea, you are already working at a startup with limited funds, or you are working at an established company, you can get started for free on everything that will be described in this book.

There is a possibility that you have one question at this point: why do I even want this? If you are not convinced by the two previous sections, then keep reading.

As mentioned, an automated build pipeline takes a lot of repetitive work out of your hands instantly. From the moment you set up automatic builds, you will benefit, because you will be notified in real time if and when something goes wrong while building your new code. No more will you go hours, days, or even weeks without noticing that the code on your versioning system is in fact unbuildable. That alone should be reason enough to want to set this up.

But the benefits do not stop there. Building is just one thing; there are infinite more tasks that you can add to automated builds. Microsoft has added a marketplace to VSTS, which enables developers to create their own tasks that can be incorporated into a build. There are already a lot of useful packages in there, but if that specific one is not there, you can just create it yourself. This enables you to run any kind of test or diagnostic on your code or app to ensure its quality.

This brings us to the next big advantage: integrating tests. With continuous integration comes testing. While unit testing is probably the first type that comes to mind, you can also integrate functional tests with Xamarin Test Cloud to test your app on thousands of physical devices. This way you can ensure that with each check-in the quality of your software is at least as good as it was before (and ideally the quality has gone up!).

With an automated build pipeline, you get all of this integrated into one place where you can consolidate all the results and build dashboards to inspect the state of your app with just one glance.

When you have this all worked out, then why not do the same for delivering all this to your users? Constructing this process is less work than setting up the automatic builds but takes a lot of work out of your hands nevertheless. To clarify, Figure 1-1 shows an ideal situation.

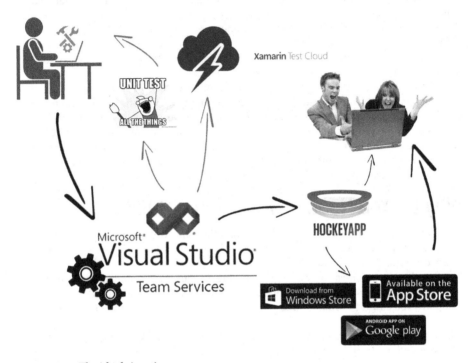

Figure 1-1. *The ideal situation*

In the top left, there is you, working on code and creating great apps. Whenever you are ready, you check your code into VSTS, which will trigger a build. In that build, your app will be compiled to see whether it still works. When it does, the unit tests you have in place will run. If everything is still OK, your app is transferred to Xamarin Test Cloud, and the automated UI test scripts are executed. If anything goes wrong at this point, it will be reported to you.

In that case, you can fix it, and the whole cycle will start again.

If all the builds and tests finish successfully, the resulting app will be released to HockeyApp. Depending on how you want to configure things, you can send your app to users from there, which can be testers of your company, and then gradually roll it out to several other groups. If and when all of these groups approve, you can send it to the actual stores. The final step in the upper right of Figure 1-1 is what it is all about: ecstatic users who love you.

If you have published apps before, you know how much work it can be. It includes identifying all the test users, making sure the right people get the right version, uploading a separate version for each platform, and compiling all the gazillion different icon sizes and screenshots to go with it.

Then, when you finally wrestle through that whole process and decide to send your app to production, you wait for the review process to complete, which can take days before showing up in the app store.

No more! You go outside of the normal app stores with HockeyApp so you can deliver your test versions in a unified way, instantaneously, while gaining a singular way to collect feedback from your users and detailed crash reports.

Also, with the release features in VSTS, you can set up a chain of command to transport your app from environment to environment. This is a powerful tool to give only designated people control over when and where to release the app, even all the way up to production! If you set up VSTS properly, you do not even have to worry about releasing the app yourself anymore.

All of this can be done automatically in a repeatable way so you never forget any step, because it won't be you who is doing it. How to set up an automated pipeline and use it to your full advantage is what this book is all about.

Final Thoughts

Now that you know what continuous integration and continuous delivery are all about, you can start getting your hands dirty. In this chapter, you learned at a high level what CI and CD can do for you, learn about the terminology that comes with them, and saw a scenario to work toward. By the end of this book, you can look back at this scenario and conclude that this is what you have achieved.

In the next chapter, you will learn how to prepare your development environment to begin implementing continuous integration and delivery for your own apps. You will set up some accounts, get an introduction to VSTS, and install the prerequisites needed.

CHAPTER 2

■ ■ ■

Establishing the Prerequisites

Before getting your hands on all the goods, there are some logistics you have to take care of first. You will need Visual Studio Team Services (VSTS), which is where all of your processes will start from. VSTS also consolidates your results into one convenient and clear overview for you.

If you already have a VSTS account, you can use that one. If you do not have one, you will find out how to set one up in this chapter. While some other accounts may be necessary, you will set them up in later chapters when necessary.

Setting Up a Visual Studio Team Services Account

To set up a VSTS account, you will need a Microsoft account. Creating one is beyond the scope of this book but should be pretty straightforward. Visit https://www.microsoft.com/account to get one. You should just have to click through a few screens, entering your information, like you would expect from any Microsoft product.

Once you have a Microsoft account, go to https://www.visualstudio.com/team-services/. If you want to see for yourself what VSTS has to offer, you can scroll through all the information there. But what you are after is the button in the top right called Free Account.

Like I promised, the account is absolutely free, which is pretty amazing once you find out what it has to offer you. Of course, free always means free to some extent." There are limits. For instance, you can invite up to five people to work with you on one account, so when your team grows to more than that, you will be charged for each user you want to add.

Note that if you or the person you want to add to your account is lucky enough to have a (company) Microsoft Software Developer Network (MSDN) subscription, that user will not count toward the limit of five. Therefore, if your company has a Microsoft partnership with an accompanying MSDN subscription, you can probably use VSTS without worrying about the user limit.

Further, there are some other limits that have to do with the computing minutes you can spend on load testing and hosted, automatic building. For more information about this, refer to the information available at https://www.visualstudio.com/team-services/pricing/.

© Gerald Versluis 2017
G. Versluis, *Xamarin Continuous Integration and Delivery*,
DOI 10.1007/978-1-4842-2716-9_2

At the time of this writing, paid accounts start at $30 per month, which gives you ten users on your account. This, however, does not remove the limit for shared services such as build agents, and so on. These can be purchased separately, and prices per month could rise very quickly. However, since I've been using VSTS, I have not had a need for a paid account.

Let's get back to creating your account. In Figure 2-1 you see what the web site looks like at the time of this writing. Web sites do tend to change from time to time, so what you see might differ from Figure 2-1, specifically, the position of the Free Account button.

Figure 2-1. *Visual Studio Team Services web site, where you can sign up for an account*

After clicking the Free Account button, you will need to log in with your Microsoft account, after which a new screen will appear, as shown in Figure 2-2. On this screen, the most important thing you must do is pick a name for your VSTS account. The name will result in your own subdomain on the `visualstudio.com` domain.

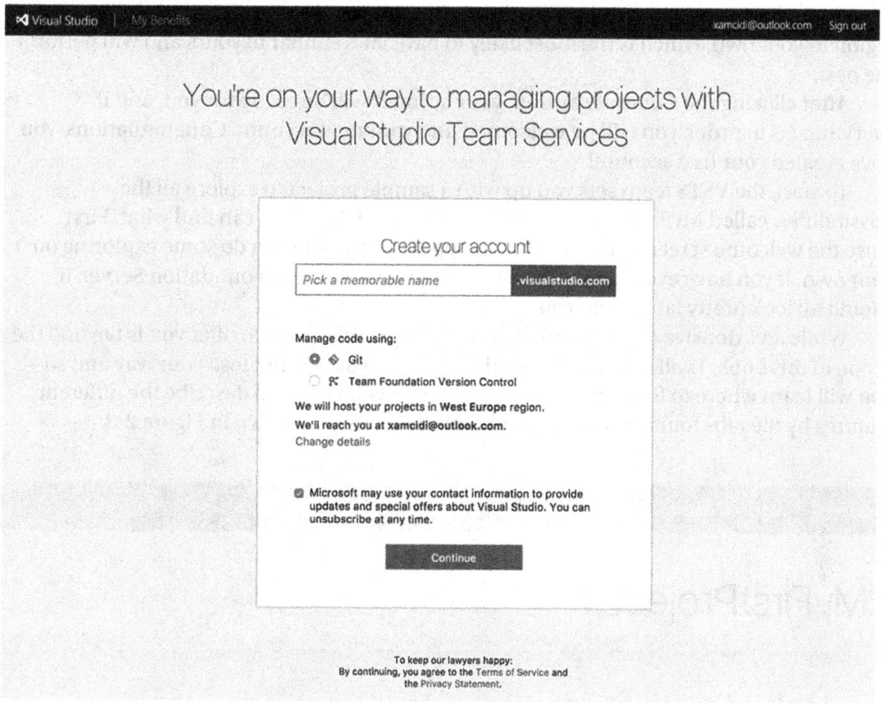

Figure 2-2. *Configuring your VSTS account*

A meaningful name will probably have to do something with you or your company. Of course, the name has to be available. Also, keep in mind that this will be the place where you will host multiple projects and apps, so do not name it after a single project.

For this book I will use the name xamcicd, which stands for Xamarin Continuous Integration and Continuous Delivery.

You will also notice that you have to choose between Git and Team Foundation Version Control (TFVC). While this seems like an important choice, you can use them both within one VSTS account. You can choose per project which one you want to use, so this is more like a default setting to get you started.

Moreover, you can set the region where the VSTS account and repositories will be hosted. While this is a technicality, it can be important if you are concerned with privacy laws and how your code is protected under these laws. Another factor is latency. If you choose a region that close to you, responses will be much faster. For instance, when you choose a region on the same continent, the ping time will be mostly between 30 to 50 milliseconds. When you choose a region halfway across the world, this could easily be 300 to 500 milliseconds.

If these are things you value, please be sure to check out what the consequences could be when hosting in different regions. To help you choose, Microsoft has provided a information page here: https://azure.microsoft.com/en-us/overview/datacenters/how-to-choose/.

If you do not want to check up on this right now, your best bet is to choose the closest region to your own, which is the most likely to have laws similar to yours and will perform the best.

After clicking the Continue button, your account will be set up for you, and if everything is in order, you will be welcomed into your new account. Congratulations, you have created your free account!

To start, the VSTS team sets you up with a sample project to explore all the possibilities, called MyFirstProject. Let's take a look at where you can find what. First, close the welcome screen with the X in the upper right so you can do some exploring on your own. If you have ever worked with recent versions of Team Foundation Server, it should all look pretty familiar to you.

While an extensive explanation of everything that VSTS has to offer you is beyond the scope of this book, I will quickly go over the basics so you will not lose your way and so you will learn where to find certain features. As you will see, I will describe the different features by the tabs found in the upper part of the screen, as shown in Figure 2-3.

Figure 2-3. *High-level tab structure in VSTS*

While you go through the tabs, there will be some balloons that pop up to help you get started. Feel free to follow them and discover what can be done.

Another thing you might come across is preview functionality. The VSTS team has stepped up its game with continuous delivery. VSTS now deploys a new version every three weeks (at the time of this writing; it could be even faster by the time you read this), and it sometimes offers you a peek into the future. Here and there you will find messages asking you if you want to enable some preview functionality.

This also has an effect on this book. The screenshots I am showing have all the latest preview bits. Therefore, some screens might look different in your account.

Project Overview

The project overview screen is the first screen you will see in every project. When there is no code or activity in the project yet, the screen will give you some information on how you can get started. When working with Git, it will tell you how you can clone the repository or add existing code to it.

Once you have started a team project, this screen will function as an overview of the team project. If you have worked with Git before, you might know about the README.md file. VSTS supports these now out of the box. This enables you to give any developer who lands here a proper introduction to what they might find. Also, on the right is information about the number of commits, builds and releases, and so on. Figure 2-4 shows the screen from the sample project I will be using in this book.

Figure 2-4. *Project overview screen in VSTS*

Dashboards

Every project has at least one dashboard. Figure 2-5 shows you what a typical dashboard screen looks like. In this case, I have filled it with some sample data so you can get an idea of how it could look like in real life. With the dashboard you can get a quick overview of everything that is going on within your project.

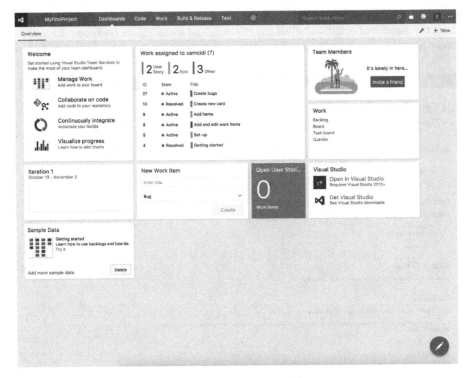

Figure 2-5. *The customizable dashboard for a typical project*

Specifically, the dashboard consists of widgets that you can add, arrange, and even develop yourself. Also, you can create multiple dashboards for one project. For example, you could create one for your work items, one for the test results, and of course one for your automated builds and releases. This way you can add several dashboards, each with its own purpose or audience.

Code

On the Code tab, you can find all the code and repositories that are associated with this project. As mentioned, this can be either Git or Team Foundation Version Control repositories. Not only can you browse through the current code here, but you can also explore all the changesets that have been checked in, show the differences between two files, work with branches, and manage your pull requests if you are using Git.

This is basically where your repository for this project lives.

Work

If you also want to keep track of your progress or your backlog, you can do that in VSTS as well. On the Work tab, you can find everything for that. Here you can also work with Scrum, Agile, Capability Maturity Model Integration (CMMI), and other templates, and you can even create your own if you require a specific method.

In Figure 2-6, you will see a backlog with the sample data I have imported.

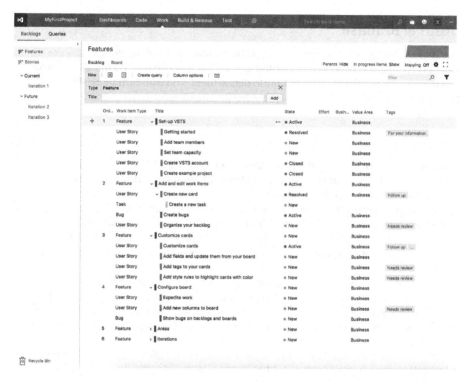

Figure 2-6. *The backlog of a sample project in VSTS*

There are several levels that you can—but do not have to—work with. As you can see, you have a Feature level, which contains low-detail features of your application. Beneath that are Story levels, which are the high-detailed user stories complete with acceptance criteria, the value area, estimated effort, and so on. And even below that you will see the tasks that can be executed by the development team.

Of course, inside all these items there are a lot of fields that you can use and customize. You can add and remove fields as you like, mark them as mandatory, and create your own way of working as you like. The same goes for the detail levels. Do you not want to use the Feature level? Just check it off in the settings and it will not be there. VSTS is flexible and powerful!

As you use more features of VSTS, the traceability between your work and code will improve greatly. Whenever new code is checked in, you can associate it with one or more work items and/or user stories. As of that moment, they are linked, and you can always trace a piece of code back to the person who checked it in and the items they are working on at that moment.

If you have any builds, releases, or tests associated, they will get linked as well, and likewise, you can trace everything back to everywhere.

Build & Release

The Build & Release tab is where the focus is on in this book. On the Build & Release tab is everything you need to set up automated builds and releases. Within VSTS, builds and releases are similar in terms of how to define them. You will learn more about this throughout the book.

Builds

You can define how a build procedure should look in a *build definition*. A build definition contains all the information to create a build of a certain set of code. It consists of steps that have to be taken, which vary from basic steps like "Restore NuGet packages" or "Build solution MyFirstProject.sln" to more advanced ones like "Run this PowerShell script" or "Copy a file to this file share." As mentioned, the most necessary steps are already there, but there is also a marketplace available where you can get even more. How to find the marketplace and install something from it is something you will learn about in Chapter 4.

The build definition also contains one or more triggers on which this build definition can act. You can set it to Continuous Integration, which triggers a new build every time new code comes in, or Scheduled. The latter enables you to specify a custom schedule, including defining the time zone, on which a build should be triggered. This is ideal for creating a nightly build, for instance.

Furthermore, a build definition lets you include or exclude certain branches or folders. Also, you can work with variables, and you can configure a retention period for the resulting artifacts of your builds.

Releases

To release a version of your app, you can use *release definitions*. These are similar to build definitions. You can even use the same steps that you use in build definitions, and vice versa. For instance, does your release require you to build some code later in the project? No problem! Do you want to perform a load test after releasing your app to a staging slot? Possible!

In theory, you could even skip release definitions altogether and just add a step that uploads your app to HockeyApp immediately. So, why would you use release definitions? They offer the chain of command that I discussed earlier.

The only thing separating a release definition from a build definition is the Environments column and approval process. In this column, you can create as many environments as you like that all have their own set of steps to go through. Also, a release definition offers you the possibility to appoint certain users or groups of users that have to sign off on the release. This can be done before the release is executed or after it is done executing. So, imagine that you have an app ready and it hits the release definition. This definition has two environments: HockeyApp and App Store.

When a release triggers, it will automatically be pushed to HockeyApp. I have configured this to notify the tester in my team who can download this version on a physical device and start doing whatever a tester does.

Whenever the tester is confident about the quality of the release, the tester can then go into VSTS and the release will be sitting waiting for approval. When it's approved, the same release will go through to the next environment, which is the app store in this case. So, you take the same version of this app, which you now know satisfies your quality expectations, and upload it to the app store. The developer is not even involved anymore and does not even have to know about it. Pretty cool, right?

Customizing Builds and Releases

There are some options in the release definition you can configure as well. For instance, I said there can be approval before or after a release, but you can also appoint one or more users who have to approve. This can be done sequentially or in any order, or it can be that the first user to approve signs off on this release and the process continues.

This makes for some powerful scenarios and can take a lot of work out of the hands of a developer. Not to mention, you do not need to share the precious HockeyApp or app store credentials with everyone; they are configured securely in VSTS.

Having said all this, one thing should stand out: VSTS is a very flexible system. This also means there is no one right way to do builds or releases. How you want to arrange a build or release is entirely up to you. You can have as many build and release definitions in one project as you like, which all have their own triggers and steps to take.

When I first started using VSTS, I created one build definition that would trigger a build every time someone checked in a piece of code. Every build would then result in a new version I could test, delivered to me through HockeyApp. When I had it all working, I was so happy! But when I started to get 10, 20, and 30 versions a day, I started to get a little less happy. So, I quickly broke up the different definitions and put some well-thought-out triggers in place to get only relevant updates while staying continuously informed on the quality of the code.

Test

Lastly, there is the Test tab, which of course has everything to do with testing. Not only can it show you information about the test results, it provides you with some pretty good tools to create test scripts and support you with exploratory testing.

It lets you create extensive test plans that can be executed on all kinds of different environments, whether automated or manual. The findings can be recorded instantly, and these results will also become part of the traceability between code, work items, and developers. You can also perform load tests with it. To make this even more useful, there is integration available with Apache JMeter.

The test suites of VSTS have some additional costs and are not applicable to mobile apps at this moment.

Setting Up a Team Project

While the MyFirstProject tab is helpful for taking a first look at all that VSTS has to offer, at some point you will want to make a project of your own.

There are multiple ways to do this, but one that is always available is to click the VSTS icon in the upper-left corner to open a drop-down menu and select "New project." Figure 2-7 shows you what the menu looks like.

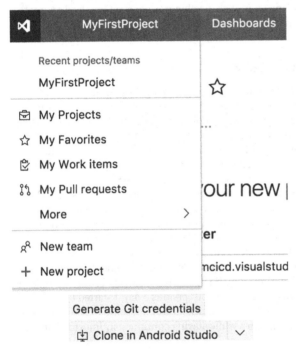

Figure 2-7. *The drop-down menu where you can create a new team project, among other things*

This is also the menu where you can switch between different projects you have created over time and access more general account settings.

When you click the "New project" option, you will be presented with a screen that lets you configure your new project, as shown in Figure 2-8. The most obvious options are the project name and description. Underneath those you can choose the template that you want to use. This influences the way your work items are presented to you and the fields they contain. As mentioned, you can even create templates of your own. If you have done this, they will show up in this list as well.

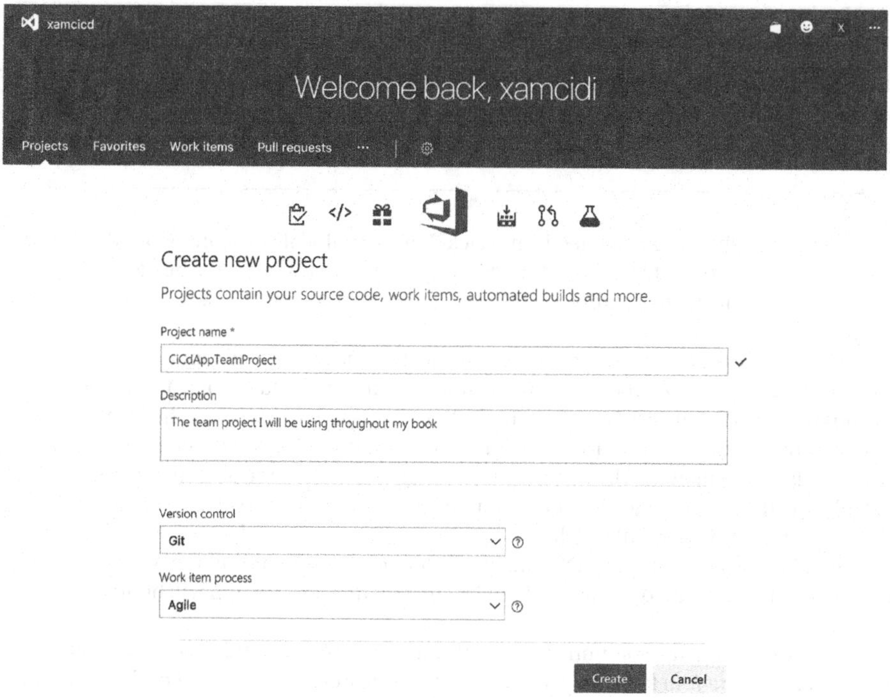

Figure 2-8. *Configuring a new team project*

As you may recall, I told you about how you can use Git and TFVC mixed in throughout the same account. Here is where you can specify which one to use. While TFVC is still sufficient in most cases, you can't get around Git anymore, which is something Microsoft has realized as well. Basically, both provide you with source control, but Git has a lot of advantages over TFVC. Even more important, if you want to connect with third-party services, the better option is Git because it is more widely supported. You will take a look at services you might want to connect to in the appendix.

When you have configured everything to your liking, click Create and wait for VSTS to tell you that your project is ready. You have now successfully created your own team project to work with!

Setting Up a Mac Build Agent

One thing that is not provided by Microsoft is the ability to build iOS projects. While this is supported, you will need a Mac to convert these projects into their native platform binaries. This is simply because Apple develops the SDK for the Mac platform, and even if you could get it running on another platform, Apple has incorporated into its license that you must compile your iOS apps on a Mac using the development IDE Xcode. Another restriction Apple has included in its macOS license is that you cannot run it virtually. However, only the SDK files are needed; you do not need to have Xcode open whenever you start compiling your app.

■ **Tip** Whenever you update Xcode, you might need to accept a new version of the end-user license agreement (EULA). This is needed for Xamarin to be able to compile your apps. So, whenever you run into some strange behavior, open Xcode to be sure everything works and the EULA is accepted.

Long story short: you will need a physical Mac machine if you want to build iOS apps. If you want to do this in an automated way, you have two options: buy a (cheap) Mac that you dedicate to building your source code or subscribe to a service that does this for you.

The latter can, for instance, be done with a service like MacinCloud (www.macincloud.com/). It offers a dedicated machine that you can use for just this purpose. It has various pricing plans, including a pay-as-you-go one. While this is a pretty good option if you want to try it first without investing too much money up front, it also has one main disadvantage: you do not get full control. You will not get administrative privileges on the machine, and you will not be able to install any software updates you might need.

So if Xamarin updates its SDKs and you integrate them into your app, you will have to wait for MacinCloud to update its Xamarin installation so your app will build on its systems successfully.

Before covering the solution I will use throughout the rest of this book, I should mention that there *is* in fact a way to use a hosted Mac machine for free. For this, you can resort to the services of Bitrise, which you can learn more about in Appendix A.

To be complete and assuming you want to be in full control of your build process, I will describe the more flexible—but more expensive—option, which is to buy the cheapest Mac you can find (of course, a more expensive one will work as well) and set that up as a build agent.

The Mac will not need too much computing power because it will only wait for a request to come in from VSTS, receive the source files, build the app, and send back the results. These are not the most intensive tasks a computer can do, so any Mac that can run the latest macOS should be able to function as an extension to your VSTS setup.

The only real requirements are that it is connected to power, it is connected to the Internet with a good network connection, and it is always on. You probably want to install some remote network controlling tool on it so you can access it without a screen or mouse and keyboard attached to it physically.

Setting up the agent is then really simple; actually, everything you need is right at your disposal from within VSTS.

From within any project in VSTS, find the cogwheel in the upper navigation bar. If you click it, you will be taken to the settings page. Then find the "Agent queues" tab. Here you will see that there are already three queues at your disposal (Figure 2-9): Default, Hosted, and Hosted Linux Preview.

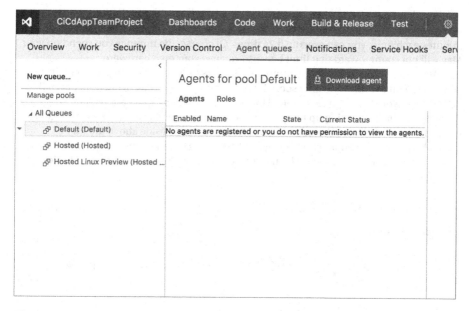

Figure 2-9. *Agent queues in VSTS*

The concept of agents and queues probably requires a bit of explanation. As part of the free VSTS account, you also get 240 build minutes in the hosted queue. This means this pool with agent machines is made available to you on Azure, but you share the pool with everyone else who has a VSTS account. Do not worry; this does not mean you have to wait endlessly for someone else to complete his build, but it does mean you do not have any control over it. It is set up with all the requirements you could think of in terms of the .NET ecosystem. (You can find a complete list of the installed SDKs and tools installed on the hosted machines at https://www.visualstudio.com/en-us/docs/build/admin/agents/hosted-pool#software.)

Whenever you queue a build (or when this is done automatically), it will find the first available agent machine that is able to build your project.

Because you have a specific requirement for building iOS apps, which is not provided in Azure or in any other way, you need to provide an agent to fulfill this requirement yourself.

If there are any other requirements you have that cannot be satisfied by the free, hosted agents, you can set up an agent for that as well, but note: another limitation of the free VSTS account is that you can have *one* self-hosted agent linked to your VSTS account. Of course, you can have many more, but only if you are willing to pay for an account.

You can, however, do it the other way around: you can use your one Mac machine to serve as an agent for multiple VSTS accounts. For this you just copy the agent binaries to another folder and run another instance with its own working folder, and so on. It will not be described in-depth here, but it might be useful to know that it can be done.

Another limitation if you are using the hosted agents is that you have the 240 minutes each month as mentioned earlier. So if you have one build definition that takes ten minutes each time, you can execute it 24 times. Of course, the minutes you spend on your Mac will not count toward that limit because you use your own hardware.

Also, unless you have a large number of projects or unless they start to get really big, you will not hit the limit any time soon. Luckily, you can specify an agent pool per build definition so you can balance your load between the different application types.

Let's get back to setting up things on your Mac. On that Mac navigate to the "Agent queue" tab and click the "Download agent" button in the left side above the list of available queues. After doing that, a page will appear that walks you through the process, as shown in Figure 2-10. If you do it on the Mac, it has already detected that and selected the right tab for you.

Figure 2-10. Instructions on how to set up your Mac build agent

Depending on your preference, you can run it as a stand-alone application, which is probably a good scenario to start from, but it is recommended to eventually run it as a LaunchAgent, which is the Mac equivalent of a Windows service. The agent will start automatically when the system is restarted.

Just follow the instructions provided by VSTS. It basically comes down to downloading the agent, running it, and entering the right connection information for your VSTS account. That is it!

If everything works out, you will see the agent in the "Default queue" list on the "Agent queues" tab shown in Figure 2-9.

While the connection is now made between your on-premise build agent and your online VSTS account, you still need to load it with the necessary tools to build your iOS apps, which is exactly what you will do in the next sections.

▩ **Note** To be able to compile your app, the source code needs to be transferred to the agent that is going to perform the build. In the case of hosted build agents, this means you are sending your code up to Azure to machines that you do not control. While Microsoft handles your source with care, it is something to consider discussing with your client.

Installing Xcode

As you probably know, Xcode is the development suite from Apple that allows you to develop iOS applications with either Objective-C or Swift. Xcode is mandatory to compile an iOS app even if you are using Xamarin.

As Xcode is not installed by default in a fresh macOS installation, you have to install it yourself manually. Luckily this is not a hard thing to do. Just find the App Store on your Mac and search for *Xcode*. Figure 2-11 shows the Xcode page in the App Store. In the top-left corner click the Install button; you may have to log in with your Apple ID.

Figure 2-11. App Store Xcode listing on the Mac build agent

Depending on your Internet connection, it might take a while to download and install because it is a few gigabytes in size.

Once it has downloaded and installed successfully, make sure you start it at least once to accept the EULA. After that, this should be the last you will see of Xcode. If at any point a new iOS version comes out, you need to update Xcode. To do this, go back to the App Store and find the screen with software updates. Just click Install from there and wait for it to download and install. After that, again start it once to make sure everything went fine and accept any update agreements if needed.

Because Xamarin uses Xcode and the iOS SDKs that are associated with that, whenever you need support for older (or newer) SDKs, turn to Xcode. Without getting into the workings of Xcode, it is good to know that this is at the base of your app compilation. So, whenever you run into something that won't compile and you cannot figure out why, do not forget there is a Mac machine somewhere out of view doing the hard work for you, where you should see whether there is something to be updated or configured.

Installing Xamarin

The last thing you need to provision on your Mac build agent is Xamarin. If you have made it this far, this will be a walk in the park.

Because Xamarin is free since Microsoft took over, you can head over to the Xamarin download web site (`https://www.xamarin.com/download`), again from your Mac machine, and download the installer from there.

After it is done downloading, run it and install it; you will be guided through the process with an easy-to-use wizard that will download all the prerequisites as needed. I suggest you download and install everything, including the Android SDKs. This means you can use your Mac to build iOS projects, which is your main objective, but it also means your Mac enables you to build your Android projects as well, which saves you free VSTS build minutes.

When you need to update your Xamarin installation, just go into your Mac, start Xamarin Studio, and have it check for updates. Just like that, you can update your agent to the latest version if you are required to do so.

If you were already running the VSTS agent, you should probably restart the LaunchAgent or restart the whole machine altogether to make sure it has detected the new Xamarin installation.

■ **Tip** When you want to build your Android apps on the Mac and you are running the build agent as a service, you might run into a problem like I did. The error message will say something like "ANDROID_HOME not set." When installing the Android SDKs, they are installed into your user account, while the service account will run on a machine account. Therefore, the Android SDKs will not be found on the system when building. To overcome this problem, take a look at this StackOverflow page: `http://stackoverflow.com/questions/37890362/android-home-not-set-vsts-agent-running-as-service-on-os-x`.

Final Thoughts

In this chapter, you learned how to set up your own free VSTS account. I went over the basics with you to give you an idea of everything that is possible with this powerful suite. Besides build and release management, on which we will be focusing, there is a lot more to explore, and I invite you to take some time to do so if you have not done that already.

With the basic understanding of VSTS in hand, I have established the prerequisites needed to get to the ultimate goal: automated builds and releases for your app.

In the next chapter, you will start looking at creating builds. You will learn what build definitions are in detail, what they do, and how you can start assembling your own.

CHAPTER 3

Creating Your First Build

Now that you have seen how to set up your VSTS account and you have learned some global things about how to use it, it is time to dive a bit deeper.

This chapter will start with a more in-depth look of what VSTS has to offer you, especially in the building and releasing area. After that, you will learn how to create your first build definition.

I will demonstrate all this with an example app that I have created for this book. The code of this app is not relevant and will not be shown in the book because it does not do anything of interest. It was merely to show you some real-life screenshots of how VSTS works.

Introducing Visual Studio Team Services

As you now know, VSTS is a lot more than just a code versioning system. While this book will focus mainly on the automatic building and releasing parts of the tool, I will go a little deeper into some other aspects as well to give you a better understanding of how certain features work together.

The sample app I have created is named CiCdApp, and the team project I have created for this app is called CiCdAppTeamProject. Your naming is, of course, entirely up to you; I have chosen these names so you can easily distinguish when I am talking about the app and when I am referring to the team project.

I am going to assume that you know how to add your project and code to a team project because this is beyond the scope of this book, so I'll skip ahead and assume you have your code stored in your team project. If you do not know how to do this or want to access some more in-depth documentation on VSTS, please refer to https://www.visualstudio.com/en-us/docs/overview.

You can now go into the Code section of VSTS and see everything that is stored right now, as shown in Figure 3-1.

© Gerald Versluis 2017
G. Versluis, *Xamarin Continuous Integration and Delivery*,
DOI 10.1007/978-1-4842-2716-9_3

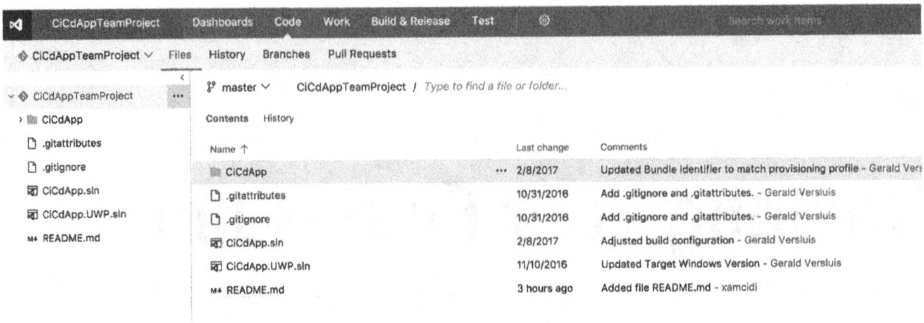

Figure 3-1. *All the code stored in the Git repository on VSTS*

The situation in Figure 3-1 may differ a bit if you do not use Git for your code versioning. On the left side you can see the folder structure of the repository for this team project. You can navigate through this folder structure like you would in any other Microsoft product: you click the nodes to open files/folders, and on the right side you click a file to view its contents.

From this view you can also get the history of your files. Here you can see all the commits that have been done, all the way back to when you started using VSTS. You can see what comments were entered, who did the commit when, and what files were changed and/or added. If files were changed, you can view the difference between versions, whether the difference is between commits or between a specific commit to the current version.

You can also see all the different branches that have been made. Note that this is specific to using Git. Again, you can see the history, commits, and differences between all kinds of files, and the possibilities will probably grow as Microsoft adds features. Figure 3-2 shows you what the screen looks like when browsing through previous commits.

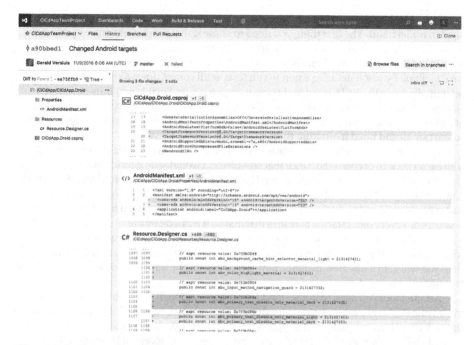

Figure 3-2. *Comparing files between commits in VSTS*

Another feature specific to Git as a versioning system is a *pull request*. For example, say you take the code from a specific branch in the repository that was created by a colleague and *branch* it, meaning you create your own copy of that code. Then you start working on improvements or extensions. Whenever you are happy with the result, you can do a pull request to the original author, meaning you request that the original author "pull in" your changes. This stimulates working together on the same codebase and crowd-sourcing the development of code in a simple and conflict-free way; you can even translate this to GitHub and have every developer in the world join in.

These pull requests can be managed directly from the VSTS web interface, whether you want to create a pull request or accept incoming pull requests by others. While you are doing so, you can compare between commits and branches and see whether you should merge the changes into your repository.

Microsoft is continuously working to make VSTS an even better product, so you will continue to see more features added over time.

Creating a Build Definition

Let's get started on what this book is all about: creating automated builds. As you may recall, this is done by putting together *build definitions* in VSTS. A build definition contains everything needed to create a build from a set of code. It has all the steps that the code needs to undergo, the triggers on which code will be built, and which repository the code needs to come from.

Before looking at how you can construct one yourself, there are a few things you need to understand. The first thing you need to know is that there is not one way to create them all. Every developer and every company will create definitions differently. There is no best way to trigger a build that is pushed to HockeyApp, and there are no rules that you have to abide by when defining when to run tests. It all comes down to how you want to set it up. Because the VSTS build and release engine is very flexible and thus powerful, it all depends on what you or your company's requirements are. In fact, you will not get all of this right on the first try. Implementing an automated build will be an evolving process, so start small and build it out from there to see what works for you.

When I first started with all this, I was so psyched that I set up a trigger to create a build with each check-in of code I did. Once that completed, I would send it off to a release and have that deliver me a new version through HockeyApp. Once that was done, I thought, "This is awesome—just what I needed." After a while, two good friends of mine joined the project and started to add code, which was awesome, but after I gradually started to get 10, 15, and 20 new versions every day, I started to realize that maybe it was a bit much!

Also, do not think that once you have set up an automated build that you are done with it forever. Although you can probably use it for a while once you have it right, over time you will gain some new insights, new requirements, or want to add even more features to your build.

Another tool you need to understand is Xamarin. Although Xamarin does a great job in unifying the way to create one app for three (or more) platforms, do not be mistaken: in the end, it will have to produce three different app binaries. Xamarin enables you to create multiplatform apps easily, but it cannot create one app that is accepted by Apple, Google, and Microsoft. You will still need to compile an .ipa, .apk, and .appx file for each app store, respectively. That's why I recommend creating a separate build definition for each platform. Also, keep in mind that a Xamarin.Forms app is still composed of a Xamarin.iOS project and a Xamarin.Android project. The concept of Xamarin.Forms is just a NuGet package that you can install to make life easier for yourself and to share the UI code across platforms.

It's time for some action! Go into your team project (CiCdTeamProject in my case) and click the Build & Release tab. Since you have not created a definition yet, you will see a screen similar to Figure 3-3.

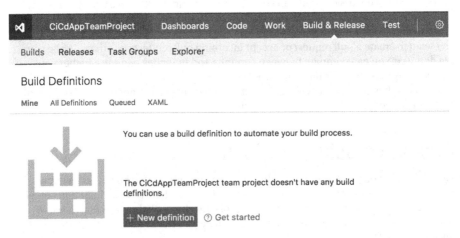

Figure 3-3. *This is the screen to start your first build definition*

Before you learn how to create actual build definitions for the specific app platforms, you will look at some basics.

Build Definition Templates

Click the "New definition" button to create a new build definition. Like you would expect from a Microsoft product, you are presented with a wizard-like interface that offers you a number of templates to start with, as shown in Figure 3-4. When you scroll through the list, you will see that a lot of the most used application types are already taken care of, including Xamarin.iOS and Xamarin.Android apps.

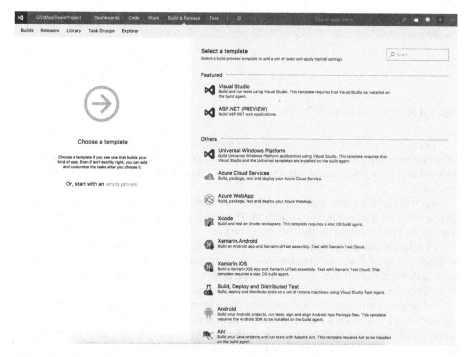

Figure 3-4. *The templates to choose from when creating a build definition*

However, the Windows app seems to be missing. Don't worry—it is not missing. The Windows app is supported by default because it relies on the .NET framework to begin with, so everything that is needed is already in VSTS.

For now, let's look at the Visual Studio template. When you select it and click the Apply button that appears, the template is then applied, and you will be taken to some predefined steps of the build definition, as shown in Figure 3-5.

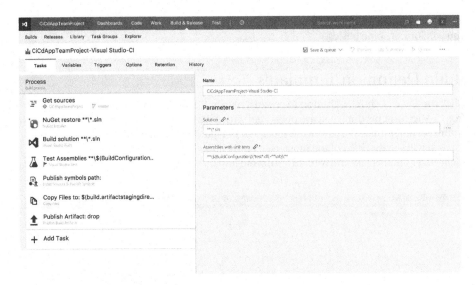

Figure 3-5. *Your first build definition*

VSTS will automatically assume you are creating a CI build and will name your definition appropriately based on the team project you are in and the template you have selected. If you want to change this, you can do so in the Process section, also visible in Figure 3-5.

Right under the name, you will see the Parameters section. These are the parameters that can be used throughout the definition. They are useful when you want to centralize some of the configuration for this build on one tab.

I'll take a moment to explain what else you are seeing in this screen. The page can be divided in roughly three parts: tabs on the top to navigate to different sections of your build definition, the left part where your *build tasks* are, and the right part where you can do additional configuration for the selected build step.

While going through the configuration, if you forget something important, VSTS will warn you by showing a red exclamation mark at the task where something is wrong. Going into the task will drill down to the configuration, and any fields that you might have forgotten or contain an illegal value will be indicated to you in red.

If you need any information on a certain option, click the *i* icon.

Build Tasks

Your build definition is made up of these build tasks. With them you tell VSTS what to do with your code in the linked repository. If you take a look at the steps in Figure 3-5, from top to bottom you see that the NuGet packages are restored, and then all solutions in this repository are built. If any DLLs with tests can be found, they will be executed. So much for the building part!

The binaries that are compiled are referred to as *artifacts*. So, the last three steps in the list will collect the debug symbols, copy all the resulting files to the so-called artifact staging directory, and then publish all files in the staging directory. *Publishing* here means that the files will be copied to the end station where you want them to be. That can be either a file share where a tester can get them or the VSTS account, where the files will land on a (secure) shared location where they can be used in a release definition.

This seems like a lot to take in, right? No worries—I'll cover most of the tasks in more detail throughout the book. There are a lot of default build tasks in there; in addition, Microsoft has added a Marketplace for these tasks, so every developer is now able to create their own. By the time you read this, a lot more tasks will be available to you.

You can add new build tasks with the Add Task button at the bottom of the task list, as shown in Figure 3-6. Also notice the link at the top, which directs you to the marketplace.

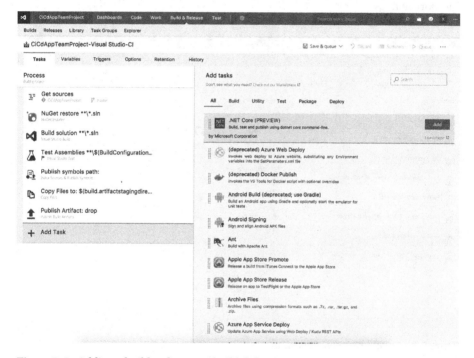

Figure 3-6. *Adding a build task to your build definition*

To add tasks to your build definition, just click the Add button after each step you want to insert. The screen will not close after you do, so you can go through all of them, adding as you go.

Let's go back to the build definition screen. Remember how I told you that the right side of the screen is for configuring the selected build step? If you look again at Figure 3-5 and you click any of the tasks under "Get sources," you will notice a section called Control Options. This section appears in every step. It lets you control some basic settings that apply to every build step. For instance, you can specify how long the step can take at maximum by setting a timeout, whether it is enabled, that it should always run whether errors occur or not, and whether the build should continue if an error occurs in a certain step.

31

All the other settings differ per type of step. I will not go over the rest right now; you will see the most common ones when you start creating your own per-platform definitions later in this chapter.

Repository

A build definition has a linked repository; this can be the repository that you created in VSTS, a repository on GitHub, any other external Git repository, or even a Subversion one. All the settings for the repository can be found under "Get sources," as mentioned earlier. When you first create a build definition, it will get linked with the repository within the team project, but you can configure some extra options afterward. Figure 3-7 shows some repository settings.

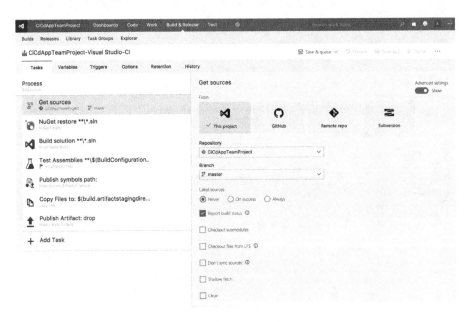

Figure 3-7. *Configuring your repository*

Besides being able to configure what repository you want to use, you can specify a specific branch that you would like to build. Also, you have the option to clean the build folder before a new build is made.

You also have the option to apply a label to the commit that is being built. While you probably will not use it with a continuous build, a label can come in handy when creating builds that are handed over to testers or even users. Labels can then help you identify what code was in the version of your app that was delivered to them. This can be really helpful when you are trying to track bugs or unusual behavior in a specific version. Please note this label will mark the source in a certain state. This will not be the version number for your app, although it can be if you configure it that way. How to update the version number of your apps is something you will learn about in the next chapter.

Below the label setting there are some more advanced features that I will not go into right now. Note that these are all Git-specific features. If you selected a TFVC repository, this screen may look different and have its own set of options. Also, as Microsoft is implementing more and more Git features, there may already be more options by the time you read this book.

Variables

Variables are another helpful feature. As a developer, you can probably guess what they do. With variables, you can specify a static name with which you can access a variable value. These variables are available across your entire build definition, in every step. So, they are especially handy when you have to use the same value more than once.

Another scenario where variables play an important role is with sensitive values. As you will learn later, apps need to be signed before they can go to an app store. To do this, you need to supply a password for the keystore or certificate. As you can imagine, you do not want to put a password in e-mail or have them in plain sight for anyone to see. You might not even want your team members to know this password.

Therefore, Microsoft has implemented secure variables. When you look at Figure 3-8, you will see a password field at the end of the list. You can provide a name and value and then click the lock icon in the value field to obscure the value. When you do this (and then save), the value is securely stored and can be used by VSTS but cannot be reverted to the human-readable form.

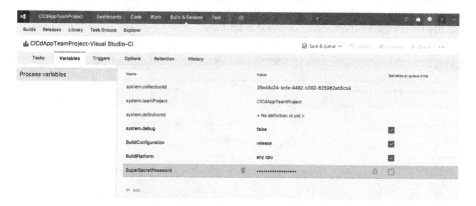

Figure 3-8. List of variables that can be used within your build definition

While you are looking at the lock icon, you will also notice the check box at the end of each line. With this check box you can configure whether the value can still be changed at queue time when you manually trigger a build. This means that when you queue a build, you will first get a screen with the list of variables that you can supply with a different value, once. So, the value you put here will be the default; when you change it at queue time, it will then build with that value, but it will not be saved.

■ **Tip** There are predefined variables to use as well. These include values about a specific build, for example, who triggered it, what the build number is, and so on. They also include values for the build agent that is building it, such as the agent name or home directory, for example. To see the list of predefined variables you can use, refer to https://www.visualstudio.com/en-us/docs/build/define/variables#predefined-variables.

If you want to put a variable in build step format, you can use this format: $(variablename). For example, if you wanted to use the SuperSecretPassword variable in a build step, you would use $(SuperSecretPassword). Variables can be used in any input field within build definitions. When the build runs, the variable will be replaced with the actual value.

Similar to variables are parameters. Parameters lack the ability to be secret and cannot be set at queue time. At the time of writing, the only use seems to be to access values of your choice from one screen that are scattered throughout tasks. To do this, go to the setting you want to access on the Process tab, click the information icon after the label, and click the Link button.

Triggers

Triggers define how the build will start. You can define here whether your build is a continuous one or a scheduled one, or both. If you look at Figure 3-9, you notice that you can use both triggers at once for one build definition.

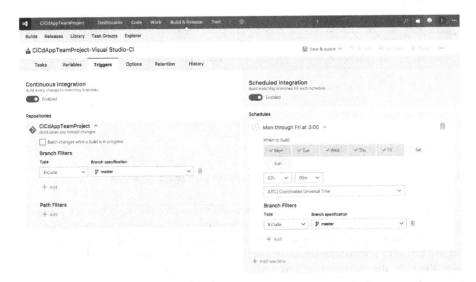

Figure 3-9. *Ways to trigger a build in VSTS*

The continuous integration build will fire every time you or someone else commits something to the repository. You have some options to filter by branch and/or folder. With this setting you can narrow down what triggers a build.

Imagine you have a repository that holds your apps but also your back-end project. If you click the CI check box and leave it at that, every commit to the apps will also trigger a build for your back end, or vice versa. This is probably not what you want because your build definitions will serve specific purposes, and thus it would be useless to build a project if nothing changed in there. With the brand and folder filters, you can fine-grain the trigger for this build definition.

The scheduled build works as advertised. You can specify one or more times when a build should be triggered automatically. This can be useful for nightly builds. Again, here you can include or exclude specific branches.

Other Options

There are a few tabs and options that I have not covered yet, such as the Options, Retention, and History tabs. While these can contain useful information, they are not crucial to creating builds. Shortly, the Options tab gives you some basic configuration possibilities, including configuring the agent queue to be used. Retention lets you specify how long artifacts that you have created and results of a build are to be saved. History shows you an audit log of who changed what in this specific build definition.

Again, they are useful, and I will handle bits and pieces of them while we go, but I will not describe them in as much detail as the rest.

Now that you have a basic understanding of all the features that are here, it is time to start looking at creating your first build definitions and queueing an actual build!

Also, in the upcoming sections, I will talk about signing your bits in order to be able to distribute your apps. Remember that you can (and should) create different types of build definitions to support different scenarios. With this in mind, you can imagine that when you're creating a CI definition whose purpose it is to prove your new code still builds, you do not need code signing. You are not going to distribute the version resulting from that build; you only use it to detect build errors and run (unit) tests automatically. The only reason I am explaining it in this chapter is so that it makes more sense and that you will know how to do it when engineering a more distributive definition.

iOS

Now let's get started on what it is really about: creating a build definition for your apps. You will start with iOS. Remember what I told you earlier: while Xamarin does a terrific job at developing your app once and distributing it on multiple platforms, when it comes down to building and distributing, it will still produce separate apps.

When you go back to the build definition overview screen (hover over Build & Release and click Build), you will see the screen shown in Figure 3-3. If you have saved any build definitions, you will see a different screen listing them.

Either way, click the button to create a new build definition, and when the screen pops up to choose a template, this time choose the Xamarin.iOS one. After you have confirmed your choice, you will see that VSTS has set you up with the bare steps again. They are a little different from the ones you saw earlier. Figure 3-10 shows what your screen should look like.

Figure 3-10. *The default Xamarin.iOS template*

You now know that red means you need to do some configuration. Let's go through the default steps first and see whether you can get this to work.

The first step is to restore Xamarin components. If you have been working with Xamarin, you may know that it has its own component store. The store offers free or paid ready-to-use components such as barcode scanners, connectors for cloud services, UI components, and much more.

If you have used these components in your app, you must enable the step to restore Xamarin components. If so, you also need to provide the user name (your e-mail address) and password of your Xamarin account. Of course, don't forget to select the enabled box. Since my sample project is not using any components, I will leave it as disabled for now. When you do not enable the step, you can also ignore the red input fields.

The most important step here is the "Build Xamarin.iOS solution" step, so let's take a look at it. When you select this step, the configuration shows up as depicted in Figure 3-11.

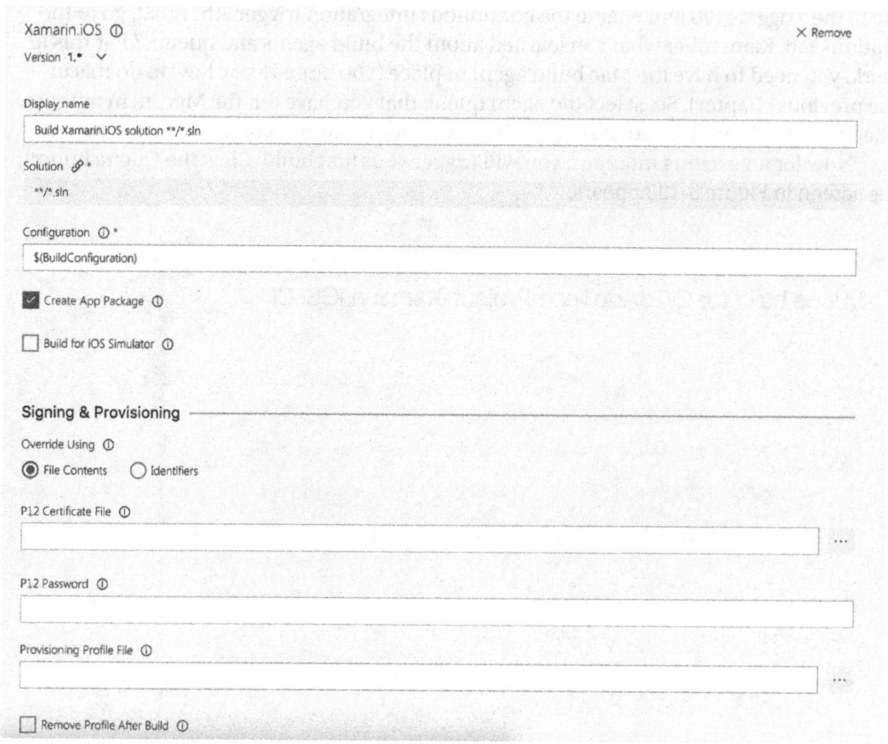

Xamarin.iOS ①   ✕ Remove
Version 1.* ⌄

Display name
Build Xamarin.iOS solution **/*.sln

Solution 🔗 *
**/*.sln

Configuration ① *
$(BuildConfiguration)

☑ Create App Package ①

☐ Build for iOS Simulator ①

Signing & Provisioning ───

Override Using ①
◉ File Contents   ○ Identifiers

P12 Certificate File ①
                                                                                    ...

P12 Password ①

Provisioning Profile File ①
                                                                                    ...

☐ Remove Profile After Build ①

Figure 3-11. *Configuring the Build Xamarin.iOS solution*

The first (and actually only) thing you need to do is specify which solution to build. There are a few ways to go about this. If you have only one solution *or* if you have multiple and want to build them all, you can enter ****/*.sln**. This is called a *minimatch pattern*. With a minimatch pattern, you can use wildcard characters to select certain files. With the ****/*.sln** pattern, it will find all the .sln files in any subfolder and build them one by one. If you wanted to build a solution under the MyApp subfolder, you would specify it like this: ****/MyApp/*.sln**.

You can also use this pattern for copying files. In that case, you do not necessarily need to specify an extension, so you can copy all kinds of files. For more about advanced examples, check out https://github.com/isaacs/minimatch/blob/master/README.md and https://realguess.net/tags/minimatch/. You can also specify the exact solution name or hit the browse button after the input field to select the right file from the repository. Remember from talking about variables that you can mix variables in here as well.

By default, the Solution field is linked to a parameter. So, either change the value on the Process tab or unlink the field by clicking the information icon after the label and clicking the Unlink button. You can now edit the value directly.

Let's start simple: select the "Build for iOS simulator" box, click "Save & queue," and then click Save for now. Before you can give it a try, there are two things you still need to do.

Go to the Triggers tab and enable the continuous integration trigger. After that, go to the Options tab. Remember what you learned about the build agents and queues? For this to work, you need to have the Mac build agent in place (you already saw how to do this in the previous chapter). So, select the agent queue that you have put the Mac in; in my case, I had to switch from Hosted to Default. Hit Save once more and confirm the save action.

Now for an exciting moment: you will trigger your first build! Click the Queue button; the screen in Figure 3-12 appears.

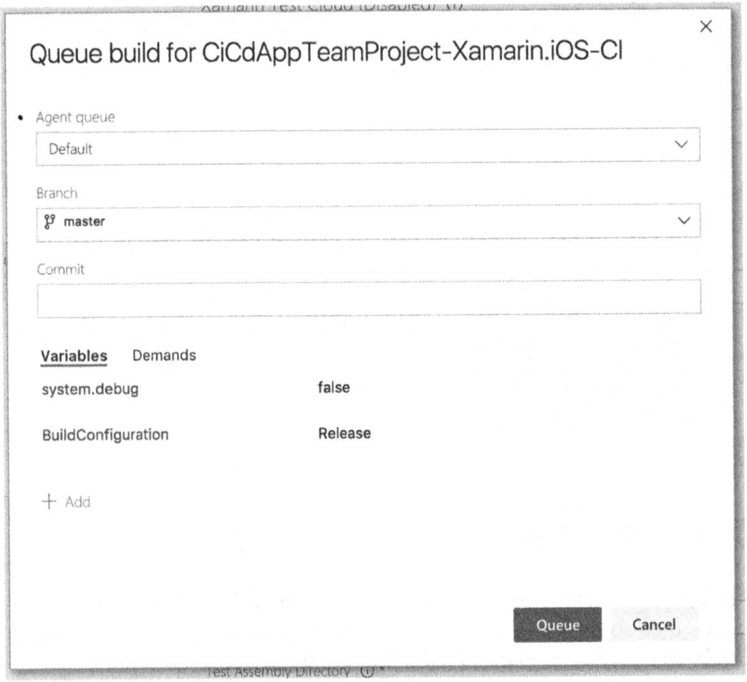

Figure 3-12. Queuing a manual build

At the bottom of this screen you can edit the values for the variables that are marked to be editable at queue time. Above that there are some other things you can do. You can switch between agent queues; since this is correct already for this example, you leave it alone. Below that you can switch to another branch and specify a certain commit that has to be used while building. Remember, everything you edit here will not be saved; it will be used only for this build. Change the BuildConfiguration variable to Debug for now, and whenever you are ready, click Queue to start the build.

If your Mac is set up correctly, the build should start, and you should see a console-like window. If it is not set up correctly, you will probably see a message like in Figure 3-13.

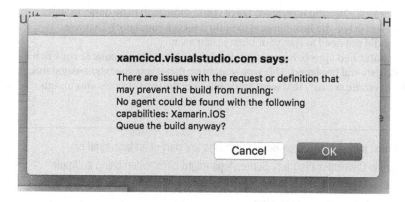

Figure 3-13. *Error while triggering an iOS build*

This can mean roughly one of two things: your Mac is not connected to VSTS for whatever reason or your Mac is connected but is not installed with the right prerequisites. Since it will be no use to try to trigger a build, cancel everything until you get back to the VSTS main screen. Now find the cog wheel and under that go to the "Agent queues" option. Check to see whether your Mac build agent shows up under the queue where you would expect it. If it does, check to see whether it is online. Also, you can check on the machine to see that you have installed Xamarin correctly and that you have set up the VSTS build agent software. Since there are numerous causes for an error, it is impossible to troubleshooting everything is beyond the scope of this book.

I will assume that everything is set up properly and when you clicked OK, the screen shown in Figure 3-14 appeared.

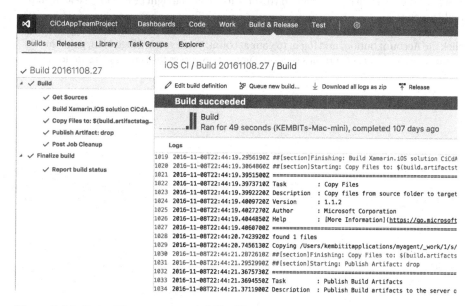

Figure 3-14. *Output from your successful build*

Hooray, your first iOS build is created! There is still some stuff to be done, though. Remember how you ticked the box that said to build it for the simulator? That was necessary so you did not need to sign your binary right away.

If you have published apps before, you probably know that the executable code that you are delivering should be signed. This way, you prove that it was you who created this, and it implements some security that way. Apple requires the use of certificates to sign your .ipa file.

■ **Note**　This next part is focused on developers who are part of an individual or organizational Apple Developer Program. Some steps might differ when using an Apple Developer Enterprise Program. You will also need to have the Team Agent or Admin role within the account to be able to follow along.

Getting the files needed for code signing your app is a bit tricky for iOS. I will try to describe it as clearly as possible, but you might have to repeat the steps a few times before you get them right.

Apple requires an app to be loaded with a *provisioning profile*. This profile consists of files that have two components: code-signing information and information about the app identity. This profile also has some information about the distribution mechanism that you use and which devices the app can be installed on.

No matter how you plan to distribute your app (HockeyApp, TestFlight, or something else), you need to create a *distribution provisioning profile*. With this profile, you can sign your application, and it will be prepared for release. The profile will contain your *App ID* and a certificate. I will now explain to you how to create the right profile for use with your build pipeline.

First, navigate to the Apple Developer Member Center (https://developer.apple.com/), click the Account button, and log in to your account. Once you are logged in, go to the Certificates, Identifiers & Profiles section. Figure 3-15 shows the screen you should see.

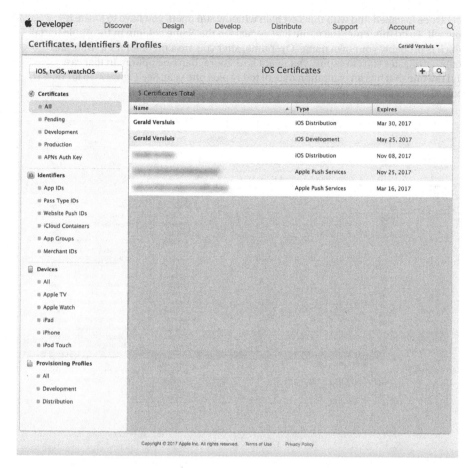

Figure 3-15. *Certificates, Identifiers & Profiles screen in Apple Developer Member Center*

Under Certificates, select Production and click the plus button in the upper-right to add a new certificate. You are now presented with a screen that asks you what type of certificate you need. If you have been running and debugging your app, chances are that you have been here before and have chosen a development certificate. This time, however, you need the App Store and Ad Hoc option, so select that and proceed to the next step by clicking the Continue button at the bottom.

In the screen that comes up, you are asked to create a *certificate-signing request* (CSR). This basically means you need to create a certificate from your Mac to identify yourself. The instructions on how to do this are displayed on the screen. If you follow them, you should be able to complete this yourself. When you do so successfully, you will then have a `.certSigningRequest` file. Continue to the next screen where you must upload this file. Do as told by the portal: upload the file, click the Generate button, and finally download the generated certificate (`.cer`) file to your Mac. Double-click the file to install it into the Mac OS Keychain; you can put it in the login keychain.

Once installed and with the Keychain window still open, you have to locate it yourself. To do this, enter the name that appears in the Name column in the Apple portal, which is probably your own name. Over time, after you are a member for a while and some certificates start to expire, you might have more than one option. In that case, find the one that has an expiration date of today plus one year. See Figure 3-16 for how I located my certificate.

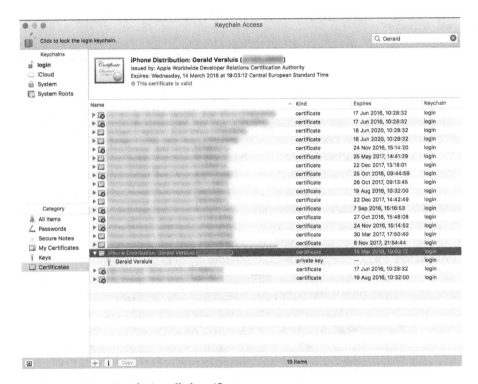

Figure 3-16. *Locating the installed certificate*

Expand the certificate like I did in Figure 3-16 and select both options (without the public key if it is there); this is important. Right-click with both the certificate and the private key still selected and select the "Export 2 items..." option from the context menu. In the save dialog, give the certificate a proper name and ensure that it is a .p12 file. When you save the file, you will be prompted for a password. Enter a password that you will remember because you will need it later. It does not really matter what the password is; it will be used in your VSTS build task configuration to be able to access the certificate.

Now for the second part. You still need to create a *mobileprovision* file. If you have not done so, create an App ID. To do this, go back to the screen shown in Figure 3-15 and in the left menu choose App IDs under Identifiers. Click the plus button in the top-right corner and follow the instructions on the screen. Enter a name with which the file will be identified in the portal and then configure the actual App ID. A prefix is already in place and identifies the team you are part of, even if you have an individual account. The suffix can be either explicit or a wildcard. Either way, it is recommended that the identifier is a reverse-domain-name-style string, for example, com.versluis.app. If you choose to create an explicit ID, it will be usable for only one app, so you'll probably use this type of naming convention. When choosing the wildcard option, you could enter something like **com.versluis.***. This way, you can use it for all your apps, as long as they start with com.versluis. Configure one of the options and proceed. Select any app service that you might want to use, click Continue, and follow the instructions to complete the App ID configuration. Make sure that this is the same ID that you configure in your iOS project. Your binary and the files needed for signing your app are linked together with this ID.

Once that is done, go back to the overview screen of Figure 3-15 once more, and this time select Distribution under the Provisioning Profiles header. Click the plus button in the top right to start the procedure. In the first screen, shown to you in Figure 3-17, you have to choose whether you are going to create a test version profile or the production one. If you are to create a test version, choose the *iOS App Development* option. If you want to distribute through the iOS App Store, choose the *App Store* option. The steps after this one are almost identical, except for the fact that when you create a development profile, you have to choose which devices are included. The devices you select at that point are the only devices that can run the test version. If you want to add more testers, you have to add the device ID in this portal (under Devices), generate a new profile, download it, and add it to your repository. I will explain how to do this later in Chapter 8.

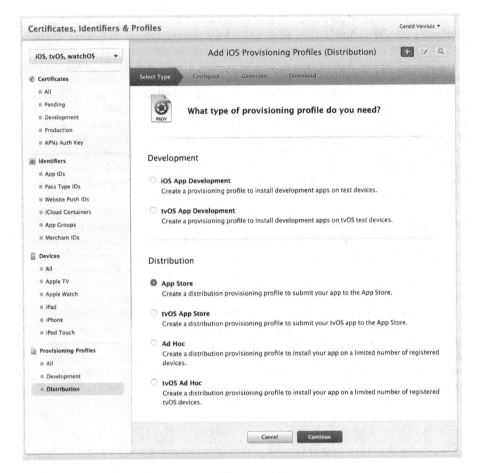

Figure 3-17. *Creating a provisioning profile*

In the screen that follows, choose the App ID you have just created (or created before) and click Continue. In development mode you now get to choose the devices to be included. In the screen that follows, select the certificate that was generated earlier. You can recognize it by the date that appears under it when there is more than one option. After choosing one and proceeding, give the profile a meaningful name and proceed to the final step. Here you can download the file to your computer, which should produce a .mobileprovision file.

Note the location of the provisioning profile, which you will be using in a moment.

■ **Tip** If you need a more detailed guide on how to create a provisioning profile, please refer to the Xamarin documentation at https://developer.xamarin.com/guides/ios/ deployment,_testing,_and_metrics/app_distribution/app-store-distribution/.

First get these files (the `.p12` and `.mobileprovision` files) into your repository. It is up to you where you put them. You can put them either at the proper platform project level or at the solution level; it does not matter, as long as they are in the repository somewhere.

Let's take another look at the build definition, as shown in Figure 3-11, specifically the section named Signing & Provisioning. There are two ways to sign and provision your app: through file contents and through identifiers. If you choose file contents, you can specify the necessary files for signing the `.ipa` file. This can be done stand-alone; you only need the password that you provided when exporting the `.p12` file. If you choose identifiers, you only have to specify some keys, and while building, the VSTS build agent will look for the required signing information on your Mac. This is probably not what you want, because this would require you to go into your Mac and download all the new signing information for each app you add in the Apple portal. Therefore, choose to use the file contents.

Now that you have the files in your repository, you can add them to your build definition. Go into your build definition and find the step to build the app. Select the Signing & Provisioning section in that step.

Figure 3-18 shows the result.

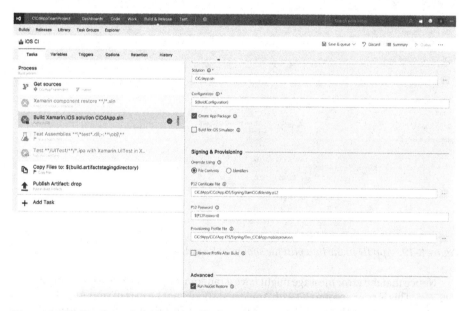

Figure 3-18. *Configured code signing for the iOS app*

There are a couple of things going on here. First, note how I unchecked the Build for iOS Simulator box again; you do not need this anymore. You want to build for actual devices now.

The most important part is going on in the section directly below that. With the browse buttons that appear after the input fields, navigate to where you put the code-signing files and select them. Then in the P12 Password field, you can either enter the password directly or, as you learned earlier, make it a variable and secure it like that.

Another thing you need to do is to go to the Variables tab and set BuildConfiguration to AppStore. This is the configuration you need to use to create distributable binaries. Save the build configuration and trigger another build.

If everything is set up correctly, this build should now succeed as well. If it does not, there are numerous scenarios possible; it is impossible to describe them all here. There are, however, two likely scenarios that I will mention.

The first is that you are getting errors about other projects in your solution, rather than the iOS one. In this case, the most obvious fix is to create a separate solution with only the projects necessary for your iOS app and build that instead.

The other common error to turn up states something like "No iOS signing identities match the specified provisioning profile (...)." In this case, there is something mixed up with the files you have generated in the Apple portal. Double-check that you have created the right certificate and provisioning file. Also check that the App ID you have in your provisioning file matches the one in your `info.plist` file. Figure 3-19 shows an example of the App ID in the Visual Studio designer for the `info.plist` file. This is available under the project properties for your iOS app. The value you are after is in the Identifier field.

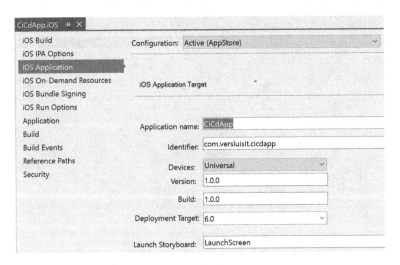

Figure 3-19. *App ID in the info.plist file shown in Visual Studio*

Notice that the error message might have a random hash at the end, something like SD67HJS. This is your account ID with Apple and should not be part of your App ID.

The good news is that the iOS build is the hardest to get right. If you got it to work, the rest will be fairly easy.

Android

You can now turn to Android. Go back to the general build screen and add a new build definition, this time with the Xamarin.Android template. Go with the default options for now, unless you now think you know what you're doing. Eventually you should see the screen in Figure 3-20.

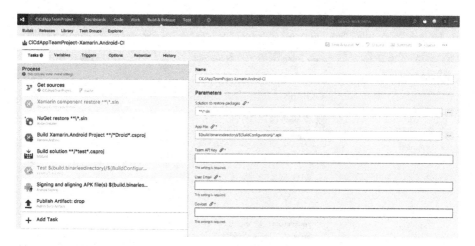

Figure 3-20. *A fresh Xamarin.Android build definition*

Like the iOS template, this also has a "Restore components" step. Since I have already handled this, I will skip it for now. Also, the NuGet step is trivial and should just work, so let's go directly to the building step. It seems a bit more extensive than the iOS one, and you do have some more options, but actually nothing new is going on here. If you do not have any specific configuration needs, you do not even have to touch this at all. One thing that does stand out is the fact that you are not building a solution in this build definition; instead, you are building a project. Make sure that your project is configured right by going to the "Build solution **.*/test*.csproj" step and disabling it for now. You can actually queue a new build right now, so let's do that. If everything builds successfully, you have produced your first .apk file!

But just like the iOS binary file, this one must be signed before you can distribute it. Luckily, this process is a bit easier than with Apple. On Android, you only need a file that is called a *key store*. To create a key store, you have several options. The hardest one is to open up a console; the easiest one is to follow a wizard, which is available in both Visual Studio and Xamarin Studio. I will be describing the process with Visual Studio, but the Xamarin Studio steps should roughly be the same.

Within Visual Studio, first set your build configuration to Release and right-click your Android project. In the context menu, click the Archive option. This will bring up the screen shown in Figure 3-21. It will immediately start creating an archive for you as well, but do not worry about that. If you were to create an Android distributable manually, this is how you would do it.

47

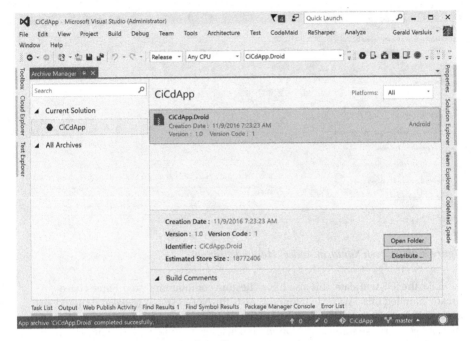

Figure 3-21. *Archive screen in Visual Studio*

Click the archive that was just created and then click the Distribute button, which will bring up a new screen that shows you all the signing identities you already have. If you have distributed Android apps before, there are probably some entries already in here.

Click the button with the plus sign near the bottom. Figure 3-22 shows you what screen pops up and how you should fill it out.

Figure 3-22. *Creating a new signing identity*

The alias is totally up to you and just a trivial name you reference it by. The password is going to be used to ensure that you can use only this key store to sign the app. Remember it for now because you will need to enter it in the build definition. When you have entered all the required fields, click the Create button; your new key store should show up in the overview. When you double-click the new entry, a screen pops up with all the details about it, and at the bottom there is a View in Explorer button. Take the file that has been created (only the .keystore file is needed) and add it somewhere to your repository so you can use it in your build definitions.

To make the signing work for Android as well, go back to the build definition and select the signing step. As you can see in Figure 3-23, I have put my key store file under the Signing folder just like I did for iOS.

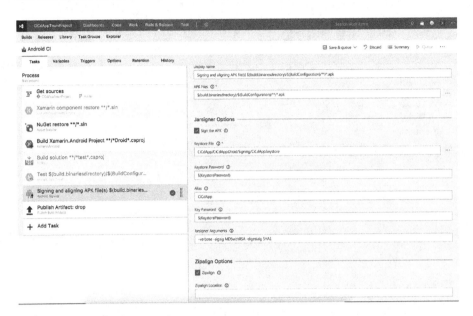

Figure 3-23. *Completing the code-signing step for Android*

Select the Sign the APK box and fill out the path to the key store file. Make sure to start at the root of your repository and use the full path. To finish, enter the password in the corresponding fields (the same password has to be provided in two separate fields) and provide the alias that you came up with just now.

Lastly, also check the Zipalign check box. While not completely necessary, this is highly recommended. If you want to distribute this version to the Android Play Store, your binary should be zipaligned. This is a specific Android optimization for the resulting .apk file. According to Google in the Android documentation, it does the following:

> *zipalign is an archive alignment tool that provides important optimization to Android application (APK) files. The purpose is to ensure that all uncompressed data starts with a particular alignment relative to the start of the file.*

When you create this build definition, you let it use the hosted agent pool. You should be able to build the Android app on both the shared build agent and your own build agent. While you have configured the Mac build agent primarily for the iOS builds, the Mac should have all prerequisites to build the Android project as well.

There are a few reasons to choose your Mac build agent over the hosted one. First, when building your own agent, it does not count toward the limit that you have for build minutes on the free VSTS account. More important, the hosted agents have a default configuration, and that is what you have to work with. If you have any special requirements, you cannot use the hosted agents. Also, if you want to use a beta or alpha update to do a build or, the other way around, if you are not ready to update yet, that is all up to you because the environment is yours to configure. As for the hosted agent, it gets updated whenever Microsoft decides to do so.

Last but not least, debugging a failing build is a bit easier on the Mac. Because you have access to the file system and all the logs, it is a lot easier to see what is going on.

Universal Windows Platform (UWP)

The UWP app should be a real breeze. Since UWP is a Microsoft technology like VSTS, this is by far the easiest definition to configure. However, you do need to do some preparation, which has to do with signing your app for distribution.

Signing a UWP project is done with a .pfx certificate. In a default project there should be a *_TemporaryKey.pfx file (* is a wildcard; the name can vary), which can be used for test purposes but not for distributing. In Figure 3-24 you can see a UWP project with a couple of .pfx files.

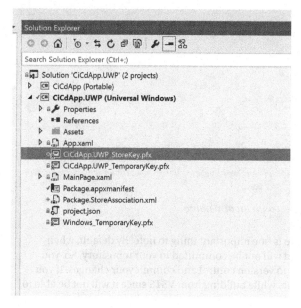

Figure 3-24. *UWP project with multiple .pfx certificates*

You can create a new, distributable certificate by right-clicking the project and selecting Store and then Associate App with the Store. You will also notice the Create App Packages option; you can use this option to create packages manually. Since you want to automate it here, choose the first option.

A new screen will pop up, as shown in Figure 3-25. In this screen, you can choose the app name that you want to associate with your UWP project. By associating it, a new certificate will be created and assigned to your app. When building the app, it will automatically be signed with that same certificate. You can create an app name from the developer portal at developer.microsoft.com or you can do it right here from this screen.

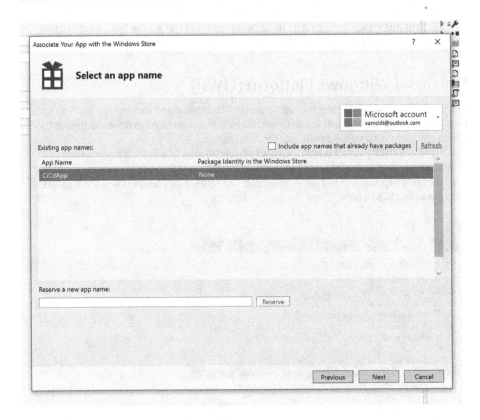

Figure 3-25. Associating your project with an app name

Once you have done this, there is one important thing to note. By default, when using Git, `.pfx` files are ignored and will not be committed to your repository. So, you have to explicitly add the `.pfx` files to version control and commit your changes. If you do not do this, you will receive errors while building from VSTS since it will not be able to find the files.

If you have done this, go back to VSTS. Once more, go into the build screen and create a new build definition, this time selecting the Universal Windows Platform template. See Figure 3-26 for reference. Leave all the options at their default and let VSTS generate the basic build definition for you. Now you should be able to try to trigger a build that should succeed! It's as easy as that.

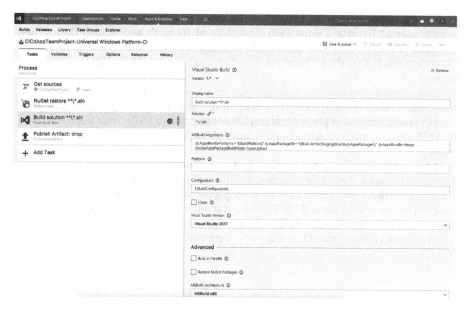

Figure 3-26. *The UWP build definition*

If the build is not successful right way, the most probable cause is that it is trying to build other platform apps as well that cause errors. The easiest way to solve this, which I have already mentioned a couple of times, is to break up your platform projects into their own solutions.

Another common cause could be that signing still is not working. Double-check to see whether the certificate file is in the repository.

When you look a bit closer at the actual build solution step, you see that it comes with some MSBuild arguments. This specifies for which platform a build is made. Actually, when you look at the value of the parameter, you can see that there are *three* platforms. These three builds will result in one .appxupload file, which can be used for distribution.

Note that you should build this solution on the shared agent queue since building UWP apps is not supported on a Mac.

Final Thoughts

Now that you know how to create different types of build definitions for each platform, play a bit for yourself. There are several optimizations that can be done. You could, for instance, create separate solution files for each collection of projects you want to build. Or you could implement different build configurations to achieve the same thing. Also, you could implement more steps to slowly but steadily expand your build definition. Do not add too much at once, so that if a build fails, you know where to look.

There is a good chance that your first build did not succeed the first time; this is perfectly normal. It can be a tedious job to pinpoint what exactly went wrong. The logs are bulky, and you will need to do some digging to get the actual errors out. To help you with this, error messages are shown in red, and the logs can be reviewed per build task that is executed.

Everyone will go about this differently, but what works for me is to go back to Visual Studio, select the same build configuration as the one you are trying to build in VSTS, and select the same solution or project that you have configured in VSTS. Since Visual Studio and VSTS are both using the same build engine (MSBuild), they should produce the same results.

Keep in mind that this is not necessarily true depending on the errors that you are getting. For instance, if you forgot to commit a file to the online repository, it will build locally, but it will not build in VSTS. So, always ask yourself what the differences could be between your local machine and VSTS to trace the source of your error. This is how you can prevent the "It works on my machine" syndrome.

In the next chapter, you will look at some more advanced scenarios and features.

CHAPTER 4

∎ ∎ ∎

Customizing Your Builds

In the previous chapter, you learned how to set up a build for each platform. You also already started with some more advanced topics such as signing your application. Now that you have seen how you can create a successful build with just the bare minimum, it is time to take a look at adding some more functionality.

In this chapter, you will learn how you can add versioning in the mix, run unit tests as part of your build definition, and customize the triggers for a build to meet your requirements. These steps are not absolutely necessary but are useful additions to your development pipeline.

Besides the build steps described in this chapter, there are a lot of others that are available and useful. Since there are numerous steps and developers can even now add their own, it is impossible to describe them all here. Also, no two development pipelines will be the same. It all comes down to the requirements you and your company have in regard to your app. Therefore, think of these as examples. After you have gotten these steps into your build definitions, you are probably good to go to figure out the rest by yourself.

Versioning

One of the things you certainly want to do is versioning because it is helpful to know which version someone is using when they provide you with feedback. That way, you create more traceability between your binaries and the code you have produced. This makes it easy to detect when a bug turns up which versions are affected. Also, making version numbers visible to end users can help them identify to you in which version a bug is found.

As you might expect, versioning is something that is platform-specific. Not only the file where you need to specify the version number differs, but it's also important to know how the different platforms handle version numbers. Therefore, I will describe the concept of the version numbers per platform and then tell you how you can incorporate versioning into your build definitions. But before I do that, I will cover the part of versioning that all platforms have in common.

© Gerald Versluis 2017
G. Versluis, *Xamarin Continuous Integration and Delivery*,
DOI 10.1007/978-1-4842-2716-9_4

Preparations

One thing that all platforms have in common is that the version number is simply determined by a string in a file. In fact, that is a good thing because you can easily replace the value as part of your build definition. The best way to do so is by replacing the value with a regular expression.

There are multiple build steps available to help you with this. The one I will be using is Colin's ALM Corner Build & Release Tools from Colin's ALM Corner. This is a third-party extension not supported by Microsoft but is really good nonetheless. You will have to get this one from the marketplace, so go to the shopping bag icon in the upper right of the blue bar and simply search for it by name. Click the Install button to add this extension to your VSTS account. Depending on whether you are logged in, you can choose to install it directly. When you have multiple VSTS accounts you can access, you will first have to choose which account you would like to install it. Figure 4-1 shows you the installation screen for this extension.

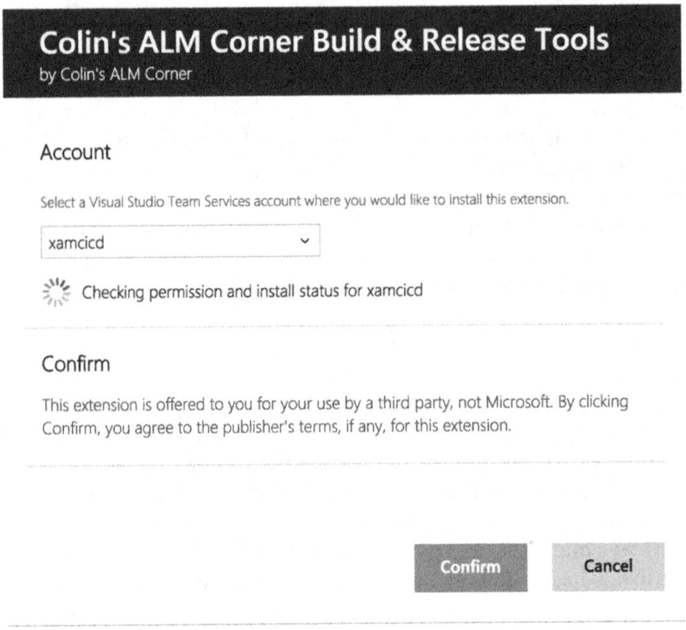

Colin's ALM Corner Build & Release Tools
by Colin's ALM Corner

Account

Select a Visual Studio Team Services account where you would like to install this extension.

> xamcicd   ∨

⟳ Checking permission and install status for xamcicd

Confirm

This extension is offered to you for your use by a third party, not Microsoft. By clicking Confirm, you agree to the publisher's terms, if any, for this extension.

[Confirm]   [Cancel]

Figure 4-1. *Installing the new extension to your VSTS account*

After you have successfully installed the extension, you are ready to implement the version numbers in your projects.

iOS

The version number of an iOS app is determined in the `info.plist` file. If you have never heard of this file before, this is the file that holds all the metadata for your iOS app. Strings to ask permission to sensors, whether your app can run on iPhones or iPads, and which iOS version to use are all specified in here. And, version numbers are specified here. Figure 4-2 shows a portion of the `info.plist` file, which shows the part about the version number.

```
77              </dict>
78         </array>
79         <key>CFBundleShortVersionString</key>
80         <string>0.5.0</string>
81         <key>CFBundleVersion</key>
82         <string>0.5.0</string>
83    </dict>
84    </plist>
85
```

Figure 4-2. *Specifying the version in the info.plist file*

As you can see, Apple uses two fields to specify the version number. While they have an extensive and official definition, it comes down to this: `CFBundleVersion` is used for development builds, and the `CFBundleShortVersionString` value is used as the official version for release builds. There is also some difference in how the version number is formatted or what the numbers mean. For more information, please refer to the official Apple documentation at `https://developer.apple.com/library/content/documentation/General/Reference/InfoPlistKeyReference/Articles/CoreFoundationKeys.html`.

About the `CFBundleShortVersionString` key, Apples says the following:

> *The release version number is a string composed of three period-separated integers. The first integer represents a major revision to the app, such as a revision that implements new features or major changes. The second integer denotes a revision that implements less prominent features. The third integer represents a maintenance release revision.*

For simplicity, you will keep the values in the `CFBundleShortVersionString` and `CFBundleVersion` fields equal.

To achieve this in VSTS, there are two things you need to do: specify a version number format in VSTS and replace the part (or parts) in the `info.plist` file. The first part is easy; go into your iOS app build definition, select the Options tab, and in the "Build number format" field you will find how the version number is determined with each build. It defaults to a format that is primarily based on today's date. It can easily be replaced with `1.0$(rev:.r)`. This will result in a version number like 1.0.1 or 1.0.99. As you have learned, a field starting with a dollar sign is a variable. In this case, it is the revision number; with each build, this number is incremented. The part in front of the variable is a static value that is just inserted as is. Of course, if you are just starting with an app, you could start the version number with 0.1.0 to indicate it is a beta or even alpha version. You can compose it any way you want and use other built-in variables, as long as you make sure the resulting string consists of three positive integers separated by two periods. For my example app, I will start with 1.0.1.

You might wonder in which build definition you need to add this. Once again, that is totally up to you. Maybe you or your company already has some policy about versioning; then just try to follow that. If you do not, maybe it is time to start thinking about it.

My guideline is to use a unique version number for all versions that go to users who are not me. That means it isn't necessary to implement this in your continuous integration build since that checks only if all builds and your tests still work. If your CI version does not build, you will know. You do not need a version number for that.

Once you are in the build definition, click the Add Task button, find the new step named Version Assemblies, and click Add. Figure 4-3 shows the result of adding it to your build definition. You can now start configuring it to work for your iOS build.

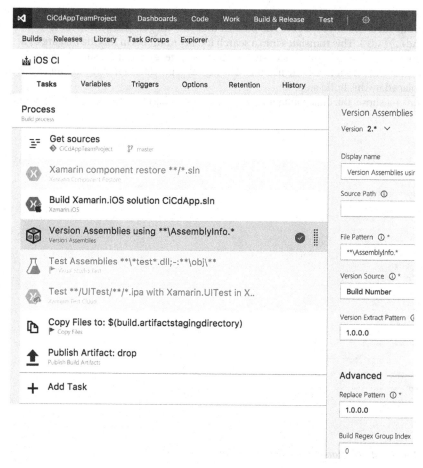

Figure 4-3. *Version assemblies step added to the iOS build definition*

The first input field wants to know where to search for the `Info.plist` file. You can enter the path directly or browse to it in your repository by clicking the browse button after the field. Find the root of your iOS project and select it. Note that the actual file is not to be selected here; only the containing folder or the folder that you want to use as the root should be selected.

In the File Pattern input box, you can specify the file or files to look for, relative from the root path you specified earlier. If you have selected the root of your iOS project, you can enter **/Info.plist**. Note that you can use minimatch to search for a file (or files) and that all fields are case-sensitive for non-Windows environments. Since you will build this on your Mac build agent, make sure you get the casing, as well as the slashes in the path, right. For Windows paths, the backslash should be used (\); for Unix (and thus Mac) operating systems, the forward slash (/) should be used.

The last thing you need to configure is the pattern you want to search for in these files, in your case, the `Info.plist`. The pattern that you are going to search for is `(?:\d+.\d+.)(\d+)`. This translates into a search for any numbers in this file that are in a 1.1.1 format. The 1 can be substituted with any positive integer. So, make sure the value in the `Info.plist` file is set to a value like this. The actual value does not really matter as it is being replaced by this build step.

Figure 4-4 shows the final configuration for iOS in the case of my CiCdApp sample app.

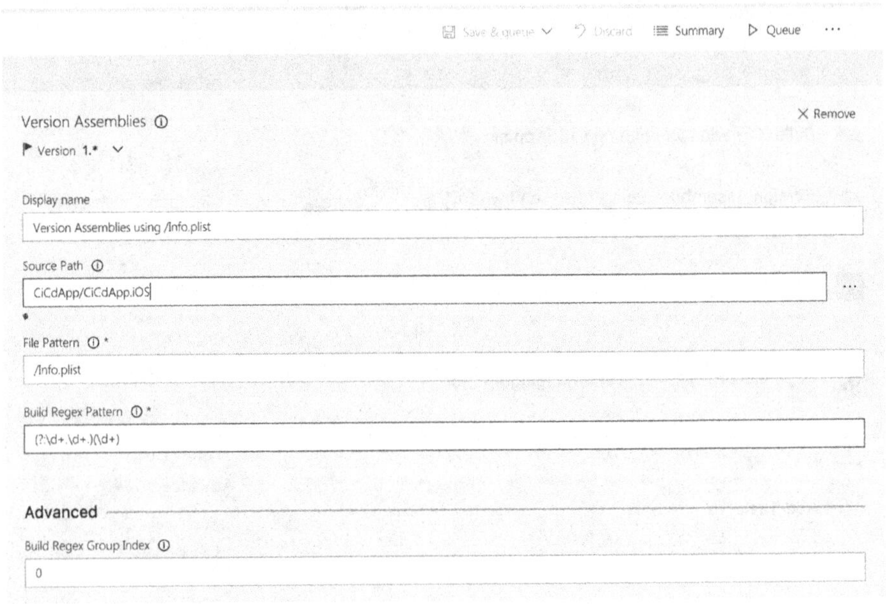

Figure 4-4. Configuration to version the iOS app

■ Note   Between starting to write this book and finishing it, there has been an update to the Version Assemblies task. If you look at Figure 4-4 in the top-left corner you can see a flag icon and a version. Every task now has a version, and you get to choose which version of the task you want to use; the flag icon indicates a newer version is available. In this example, I am still using 1.* even though version 2.* is available. Version 2.* has some minor changes, such as some preconfigured regex patterns. The configuration as I am describing here is also still possible with version 2 of this task.

When you now trigger a new build, in the output you should see how many matches have been found for the regular expression and whether they have been successfully replaced.

The only downside to all this is that whenever you feel like something more major happened in your code, you have to go into your build definition and increase the version number manually. There is no real alternative to this since you cannot programmatically determine whether any major functional changes were made.

Android

For Android, the concept is about the same; however, the version number is now in a file called AndroidManifest.xml and it works slightly differently internally. Like Apple, Google uses two fields for the version number. There is a versionCode field, which is a positive integer that is to be incremented and can be evaluated by systems to determine whether one version is newer than another. There is also the versionName field. Typically, this is filled with a value like 1.0.1 as a version number. But it is a string value, so it could also be 2.1.0-alpha or a codename like Nougat or Marshmallow. The versionName field has no other purpose than to be displayed to the end user. Figure 4-5 shows how these fields are represented in the AndroidManifest.xml.

```
1  <?xml version="1.0" encoding="utf-8"?>
2  <manifest xmlns:android="http://schemas.android.com/apk/res/android" package="it.versluis.cicdapp.android"
3      android:installLocation="auto" android:versionCode="1" android:versionName="1.0">
4          <uses-sdk android:minSdkVersion="15" android:targetSdkVersion="23" />
5          <application android:label="CiCdApp.Droid"></application>
6  </manifest>
```

Figure 4-5. *AndroidManifest.xml file showing the versionName and versionCode fields*

Furthermore, Google says this about the version numbers for your Android app:

Typically, you would release the first version of your app with versionCode set to 1, then monotonically increase the value with each release, regardless whether the release constitutes a major or minor release. This means that the versionCode value does not necessarily have a strong resemblance to the app release version that is visible to the user (see versionName, below). Apps and publishing services should not display this version value to users.

Read more about the versioning of Android apps on the documentation page, which can be found at https://developer.android.com/studio/publish/versioning.html.

The way you are going to configure this is to just increment the versionCode field for each build by using the same revision variable that you used in your iOS builds. For the versionName field you will just use the major.minor version number notation.

Go into the Android build definition, click Add Task, and find the Version Assemblies step again. Please refer to Figure 4-3 to see what it should look like. In the first input field, start looking for the folder that contains the AndroidManifest.xml file in your Android project. In the second field, fill in the AndroidManifest.xml file name. Please note the casing because it is case-sensitive. Take a look at Figure 4-6 to see what my configuration looks like.

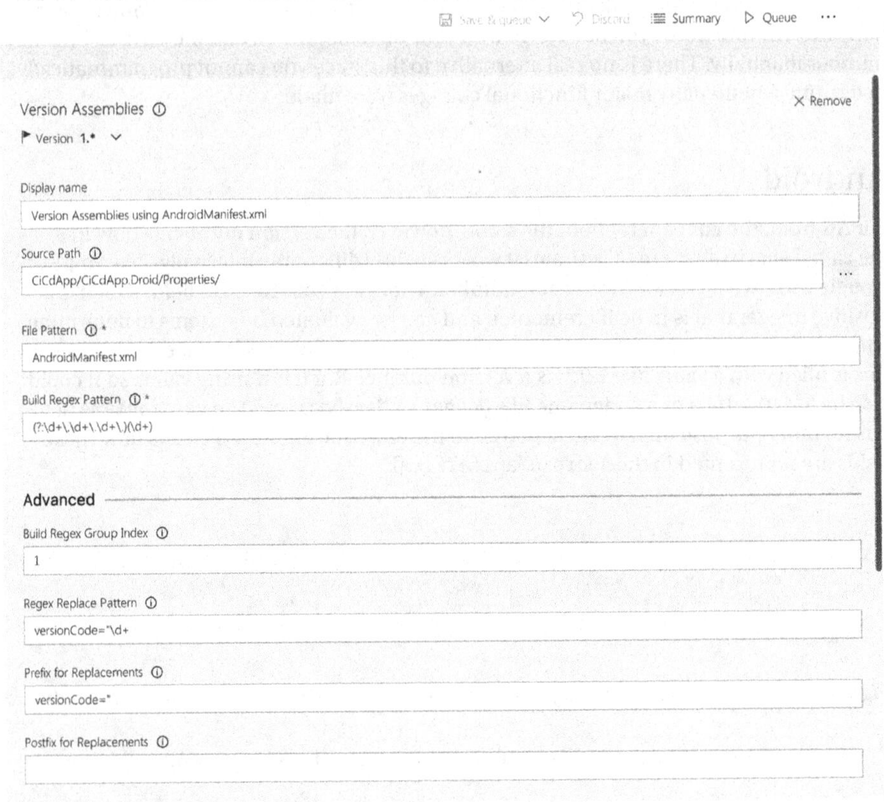

Figure 4-6. Configuring the versioning of your Android app

To finish the configuration here, you just need to specify the regular expression options to figure out what you want to replace. In Build Regex Pattern, enter this pattern: **(?:\d+\.\d+\.\d+\.)(\d+)**. As you can see, there are two sets of parentheses, meaning there are two groups in there. This effectively means you will break up the build number, which you will set in a moment, in two parts. This is exactly what you will work with on the Advanced tab.

In the Build Regex Group Index field, enter the value **1**. This means you will be using the last part between parentheses as the value you are replacing with.

Furthermore, to ensure you replace the right part, you will specify it including a versionCode= prefix. So, in Regex Replace Pattern enter **versionCode="\d+**. This will look for the versionCode attribute trailing with a positive integer value. This is going to be replaced with the revision part of your build number. Since you are including the versionCode=" prefix in the replace pattern, you also have to add it back in there. To do this, fill in **versionCode="** in the Prefix for Replacements field.

The final thing to do here is set the build number format on the Options tab. Head over there and fill the "Build number format" field with a version number similar to **1.0.0$(rev:.r)**. If you match this to the pattern you saw earlier, you will see that the value in the revision variable is the value in the second part of the regular expression. This is the number that is incremented with each build, and this is the number you will use as the versionCode for your Android app.

The versionCode field will be left intact this way. So, here you can put in your own version number and manually increment every time you think a major change has been made. You can also add another regular expression step to have the value change with the VSTS build number accordingly. I will leave versionName as is and just increment the versionCode value. This will result in version numbers like 1.0 (4), where 1.0 is the value from versionName and 4 is from versionCode.

UWP

Like in other areas, the UWP app is a bit easier than the other ones. The version number for UWP apps consists of four positive integer numbers separated by periods. Microsoft specifies the following about the UWP version number on its web site:

> *Each package you provide must have a version number (provided as a value in the Version attribute of the Package/Identity element in the app manifest). The Windows Store enforces certain rules related to version numbers, which work somewhat differently in different OS versions.*

There are some different rules for Windows 8/8.1 apps, but I will focus on just the requirements for Windows 10 apps. It is important to note up front that the last digit must be 0 because it is reserved for the Windows Store. For all information on the versioning of Windows apps, please refer to the documentation on the Microsoft web site at https://msdn.microsoft.com/en-us/windows/uwp/publish/package-version-numbering.

The version number is stored in the Package.appxmanifest file, in an attribute that is called simply Version, specified in the Identity node. Figure 4-7 shows the content of the manifest file with the Version field.

```
1  <?xml version="1.0" encoding="utf-8"?>
2  <Package xmlns="http://schemas.microsoft.com/appx/manifest/foundation/windows10" xmlns:mp="http://schemas.microsoft.com/appx/2014/phor
3    <Identity Name="Verslu.isIT.CiCdApp" Publisher="CN=A1FEB5DA-002B-48CC-AE09-A3AFA3C78275" Version="1.1.0.0" />
4    <mp:PhoneIdentity PhoneProductId="aa78c34f-7596-4796-b38e-07573b14b51c" PhonePublisherId="00000000-0000-0000-0000-000000000000" />
5    <Properties>
6      <DisplayName>CiCdApp</DisplayName>
7      <PublisherDisplayName>Verslu.is IT</PublisherDisplayName>
8      <Logo>Assets\StoreLogo.png</Logo>
9    </Properties>
10   <Dependencies>
11     <TargetDeviceFamily Name="Windows.Universal" MinVersion="10.0.0.0" MaxVersionTested="10.0.0.0" />
12   </Dependencies>
13   <Resources>
14     <Resource Language="x-generate" />
15   </Resources>
16   <Applications>
17     <Application Id="App" Executable="$targetnametoken$.exe" EntryPoint="CiCdApp.UWP.App">
18       <uap:VisualElements DisplayName="CiCdApp" Square150x150Logo="Assets\Square150x150Logo.png" Square44x44Logo="Assets\Square44x44L(
```

Figure 4-7. *Version field in the Package.appxmanifest file*

To make sure you can replace the value in this field, you need to enter a version number with four digits, in example, 1.0.0.0. This can be done either directly in the file or from the editor when you double-click the file from within Visual Studio.

When you have checked in this file, you will go to VSTS and add the Version Assembly step to your Windows build definition. The process is similar to the Android app. In Source Path, navigate to the folder where Package.appxmanifest is located and in the field named File Pattern enter the file name. The regular expression you will use is \d+\.\d+\.\d+\.\d+, in which you can recognize the four-positive integer pattern separated by dots. Lastly, go into the Advanced tab and set Regex Replace Pattern to **Version="\d+\.\d+\.\d+\.\d+**. This makes sure you only replace the value that is directly after the Version= prefix. To make sure the value that you are replacing it with will produce a valid XML attribute, make sure Prefix for Replacements is filled with **Version="**.

Figure 4-8 shows this configuration.

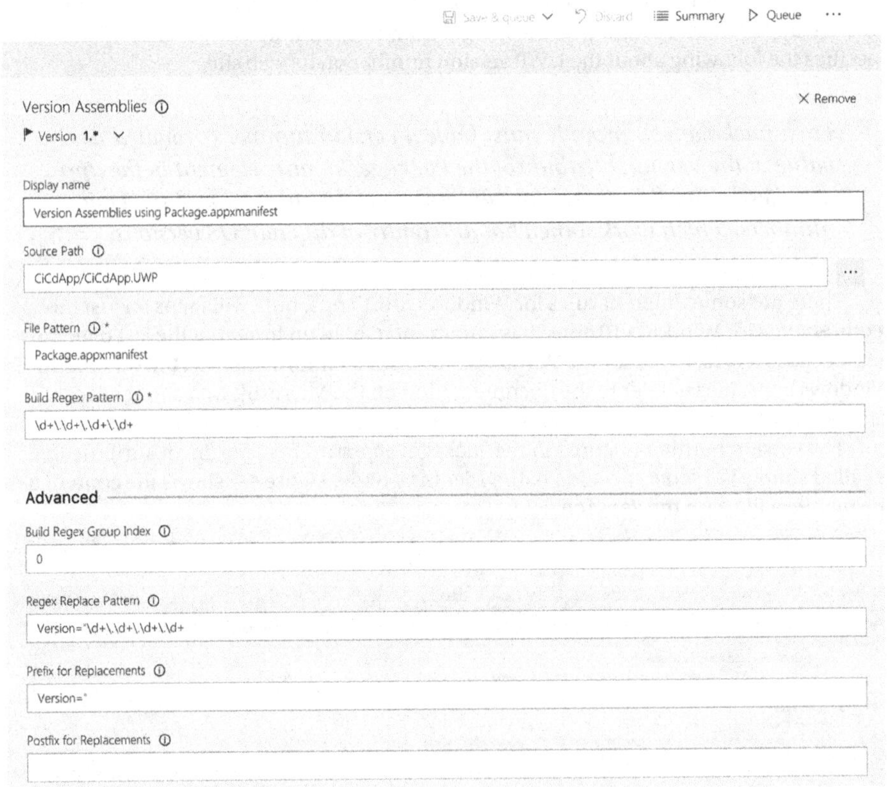

Figure 4-8. *Configuring the versioning of your UWP app*

Now head over to the Options tab and fix the build number format. Set it to **1.0$(rev:.r).0**. As you have learned, this results in a version where the third decimal is the one that is incremented automatically. As you may recall from the start of this paragraph, the last number must be a 0, as determined by Microsoft.

Save all the new settings, and when you now trigger a build for your Windows app, it will result in a correctly versioned app.

Different Types of Build Definitions

Throughout this book I will use just one build definition, which is the continuous integration (CI) one. Like I have mentioned, there is no one right way of composing a build definition. It is all a matter of your own (or your company's) requirements. It is totally up to you which components you specify in one definition or what you do or do not as a whole.

However, here are a few pointers:

- *Keep your build times as short as possible*: One of the big advantages of automated building is that you get feedback as early as possible. You will know in a matter of seconds (a few minutes at most) if something is wrong and needs to be fixed. This becomes even more important when working on one project with multiple people; when a build fails, other people cannot commit code until it is fixed.

- *Break up build definitions by responsibility*: This supports the previous point. If you try to do everything in one build definition—building, testing, uploading artifacts—the feedback cycle grows larger. Especially Test Cloud runs can become lengthy if you choose popular devices or your tests become more extensive. Lastly, sometimes it is just impossible to do everything from one build. As you will learn in the next chapter, Test Cloud can require a special build that would not be accepted by the iOS App Store. For that reason alone, you need separate build definitions.

■ **Note** When you go with separate build definitions, you probably want to have some kind of dependency between them. When build A fails, B should not be able to start, for instance. At the time of writing, this kind of behavior is not supported in VSTS. There is a ticket for it on the VSTS UserVoice (https://visualstudio.uservoice.com/forums/330519-team-services/suggestions/2165043-provide-build-configuration-dependencies-in-tfs-bu), but there is no ETA for when it will be fixed.

- *Start small*: As I've mentioned, it will take a few tries before you get your project to build the first time, especially when you are applying it to an already existing project. In itself that already proves the usefulness of continuous builds; you will immediately come across some stuff that makes it hard to build the project on another machine than your own. That is not something you want. Ideally, your code can be pulled down from the repository and buildable from the very first moment. After you get the hang of it, try to expand with the next step and the next. After that, start breaking up your different build definitions.

- *Do not release every version*: The fact that you can do continuous delivery does not mean that you must do it every time. When I just started with all this, I thought, "This is awesome; I get a testable version of every change I make." And so it happened: I created my build definition and started working. Down the road, two colleagues joined my and started committing code as well. With the build definitions still in place, I now got 10 to 15 versions every day, with every tiny fix that was committed. Needless to say, that was not what I intended to do.

- *Use the Clean option*: In VSTS there is the option to clean your working folder before a build commences. With this option the source/binaries are removed first. By enabling this option, you make sure that no files are left behind, making the build possible only on that machine. When you are using hosted build agents, the necessity for this option is not that high, as the whole machine is cleaned for you. By having a clean machine every time, you are ensured that you do not have any dependencies on something that exists only locally.

Typically, you want to have these build definitions with their respective triggers:

- *Continuous integration*: This is one you always want. It does not have to do with anything more than just building the code and reporting if it worked. You can also include unit testing in this definition, as long as the tests do not take too long. The trigger for this build should be whenever code is committed, in every branch.

- *Test*: When your tests take longer (like Test Cloud tests), put them in a separate definition. You can have it triggered, for example, every night or let it be triggered by another build. Being triggered by another build is not something that is supported by default, but there are extensions for this available in the marketplace.

- *Distribute*: This definition is just for getting out test versions. Not only does this build a binary, it will also deliver artifacts, which will result in a distributable version. When working with Git, you could work with the branch filters to let this definition get fired only when something is committed to the master branch. You will learn how to do this in the next section of this chapter.

I will cover this in more depth in Chapter 10.

Triggers

I mentioned triggers a little earlier, but I will cover them in a bit more detail here. If you go to the Triggers tab within a build definition, you will see that you have basically two options: Continuous Integration and Scheduled. As you probably know by now, the first will trigger a build every time you commit code, and the second will trigger a build at a set time (or times). There is, however, a third option, which is not visible here or in the user interface. A trigger can also be called by the VSTS REST API. With the API, you can trigger a build yourself programmatically or with a third-party system. This can also be referred to as a *web hook*, which describes the concept of triggering an action with a POST request to a certain endpoint.

In this case, a POST request to the VSTS servers holding information on the build that you want to trigger, is all that is needed. A use case for this might be that you want to use a GitHub repository but want to use the build capabilities of VSTS. In this case, you can use an API call to notify VSTS of the fact that code has been committed to the GitHub repository, thus triggering a build with the new source code.

Continuous Integration

Let's take a closer look at the continuous build trigger. In Figure 4-9 you see the screen that is used to configure the continuous trigger.

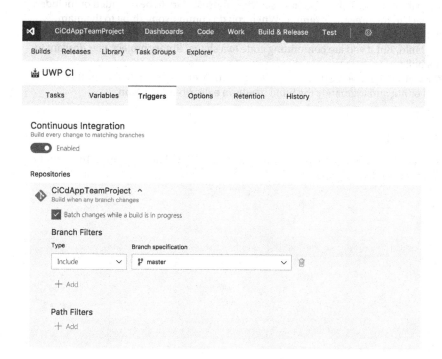

Figure 4-9. *Continuous integration trigger configuration*

I will walk you through the available options here, from top to bottom. With the "Batch changes" check box, you can do just that. When you have a large team that commits a lot of changes, this check box changes the build's behavior a bit. When a build is running, no new build will be queued until it is done, disregarding the outcome. This means all the changes by you or your team made while a build was in progress will be batched, and a new build with all those changes will be triggered only when the previous build is done. If this check box is unchecked, new builds will just be queued with each change that comes in, and they will all be handled in the order they came in.

The most important part is in the bottom part of the screen. Here you can select branches (in case of Git) and folders that are to be included or excluded for this trigger. The branch filter option should be straightforward. You can specify branches that should or should not be monitored for this build definition. So, imagine you have a build definition that builds a beta version. And, you are working with feature branches. You probably want to exclude these since you are still working on them, but you want to include the main branch. Whenever you commit something to a feature branch, nothing happens, at least not with this build definition. But when you commit to the main branch, it will build your code and produce a beta version. Please note this is true for this build definition. For your continuous integration definition, you could include all branches.

Also, to exclude—or include, of course—you can use wildcards. If you want to exclude all feature branches, you can just specify to exclude feature-*, and all the branches with that prefix will be excluded.

The path filter does the same but for folders. Here you can specify whether certain folders—within the branches you have selected above it—are to be excluded or included. Let's go back to the previous example. When you do commit something to the main branch but it is in a folder that contains the back-end API project, you do not want to trigger a build. But if you are committing code to a shared library project, you *do* want to trigger a build.

With these filters, you gain fine-grained control over whether a build should be triggered or not and ultimately the build results in a distributed version.

Scheduled

Another possibility to trigger a build is doing it at a scheduled time. Figure 4-10 shows the options for scheduled triggers.

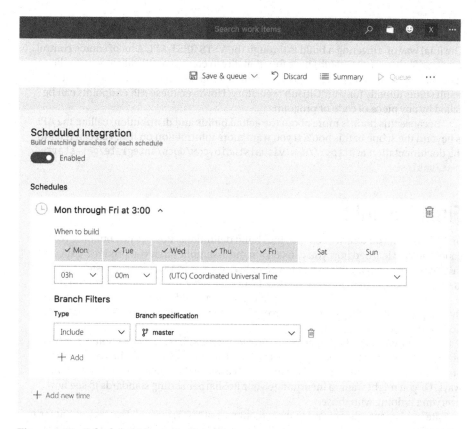

Figure 4-10. *Scheduled trigger configuration*

One recurring schedule is already configured for you. On all workdays a build is being triggered at 03:00 UTC. You can customize this to trigger it on only the days you want at a specific time. You can also create multiple schedules. For instance, if you want to trigger a build for your local team only on Mondays at night, you create a trigger and select just Monday at the time you want with your local time zone. But maybe you have a team working in another country in another time zone, so you add another trigger in their time zone, also at night but now for Friday. It is all up to you!

Just one thing to note: you can filter branches here, but the filters you specify will be evaluated for all the time triggers you specify earlier. So, you cannot have one trigger with a specific filter and have a second trigger with another filter.

One thing you might have noticed in the figures is that the continuous and scheduled triggers both have check boxes. This means you can have them both configured at the same time. Also, please note that the settings for one trigger *do not* affect the other one.

VSTS REST-API

The final way of triggering a build is through the VSTS REST-API. A lot of source control services (for instance, GitHub) have functionality to create an API call for you. In the specific case of GitHub, it even has deeper integration, and you can also see the build result status directly for your GitHub repository. However, these API endpoints can be called by any piece of code or program.

Because this book is more about the actual builds and distribution, calling the API is beyond the scope of this book. If you want more information on this, you can refer to the documentation at `https://www.visualstudio.com/docs/integrate/get-started/rest/basics`.

Final Thoughts

In this chapter, you took a deep dive into build definitions. Besides just building your code, you also learned how you can version the assemblies that you produce. Especially in an enterprise environment where you deliver your apps to a group of testers, having a good versioning system in place is crucial since the testers will want to report on it.

Furthermore, you looked at how you can trigger builds and fine-tune those triggers. By composing the right filters, you prevent unnecessary builds and versions that might not contain the code you want.

The number of tasks that apply to mobile apps is still (relatively) limited, but there are of course some other useful use cases that I can think of, one of which is the use of SonarQube. SonarQube can assist you with measuring the quality of your code in many ways. Or you might want to incorporate your ReSharper coding standards to see how everyone is doing with those.

Before I go into the release management part of VSTS, you will first look at Xamarin Test Cloud. In the next chapter, you will learn what Test Cloud is, how you can benefit from it, and how to add it to your builds.

■ ■ ■

CHAPTER 5

Creating and Running Tests with Xamarin Test Cloud

In addition to regular unit tests, there are numerous other types of tests that can be useful in their own way, such as automated UI tests. You could, of course, write a lot of test scripts and go through them each time you release a version. If your app is small and you are the only developer, that could work fine. But as your app starts to grow, you are supporting more and more platforms, and as your development team grows, doing these kinds of tests becomes undoable by hand.

Luckily, this is something that can be automated. Xamarin does a great job with this. You can create test scripts right in the code and run them automatically locally or send them over to Test Cloud and have them run for you on actual physical devices.

A First Look at Xamarin Test Cloud

Xamarin Test Cloud was first introduced in 2014. At that time, it launched with support for more than 1,000 physical devices. Xamarin also conducted a survey that pointed out that more than 80 percent of developers were relying on manual testing. At the same time, 75 percent of those developers declared that the quality of an app is the top priority when developing one. Thus Test Cloud was born.

In a warehouse in Denmark, Xamarin now has more than 2,000 physical (non-jail-broken) devices for you to test with, while still adding roughly 100 each month. These tests run fully automated, and the results can be incorporated into your favorite systems.

All the results come with all the details you, as a developer, want to know when a test fails. Statistics about memory, duration, and CPU usage are right there. But as an image speaks more than a thousand words, you can also see full-frame screenshots of every step of the way. Xamarin is even working on being able to show you a short video clip of the steps leading up to the failure of your test. And if all of this was not enough already, Xamarin has announced a feature that gives you the ability to get control over one specific device. So, when your app shows a bug only on a Micromax Canvas Knight Cameo running Android 4.4.2, you can upload your app, "grab" that device, and start a remote debug session on it.

© Gerald Versluis 2017
G. Versluis, *Xamarin Continuous Integration and Delivery*,
DOI 10.1007/978-1-4842-2716-9_5

All of this makes for a tremendous powerful test suite. Think about it: Android alone has 24,000 unique device types, and iOS has 20 hardware and OS configurations per this Test Cloud data sheet: `http://cdn1.xamarin.com/webimages/assets/Xamarin-Test-Cloud-Datasheet.pdf`. If you want to cover 75 percent of the market share in the United States alone, you will need about 134 devices. I do not know about you, but I do not have the money or the time to do that.

Enough about how wonderful Test Cloud is. "Surely, it is not all that perfect," I hear you thinking. It pretty much is, but it cannot do everything. There are a few limitations: you cannot work with anything Bluetooth related, there is no camera support, and testing only happens over Wi-Fi. Most importantly, currently there is no support for Windows Phone.

Also, it is a bit expensive. Contrary to most of the other products I describe in this book, Test Cloud has no free tier to start from; it does offer a 30-day free trial, though. After that, prices start at $99 per month for unlimited apps on one concurrent device for one hour a day. This means if your test takes ten minutes to complete, you can do six tests and then must wait another day to complete another six. If you wanted to have more concurrent devices (for instance, two), you could run two tests side by side and do it in half the time, effectively giving you the ability to run more tests in less time. See Figure 5-1 for the explanation on the Xamarin web site.

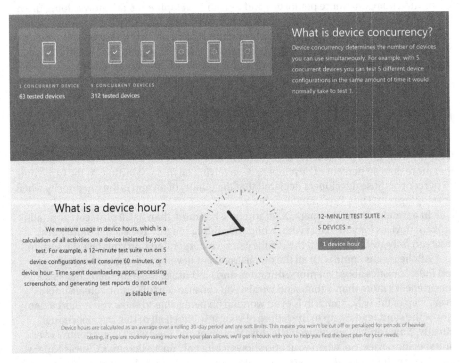

Figure 5-1. *Explanation of concurrency and device hours on the Xamarin Test Cloud web site*

For $380 per month, you will get three concurrent devices and five hours per day, and there are plans that give you even more.

As mentioned, this can come across as a bit much if you are just a single developer working from home. But as your app starts to grow and you find yourself spending more and more time hunting down bugs whenever a user reports them, you will soon find this is well worth the money. If you are an MSDN subscriber, you get a 25 percent discount. Also, if you enroll in Xamarin University, you will get some "free" hours to spend.

If you do have some test devices lying around, you can also run tests locally. This way you can still benefit from some time gained while doing automated regression tests. (Although this is possible, it will not be described in this book.)

All this greatness can be integrated in the continuous pipeline, as you will see later, and the best thing is it is not even exclusively for Xamarin apps! If you have apps lying around written in Java or Swift or whatever, you can also test them automatically using Test Cloud.

Creating UI Tests

Creating the actual tests can be done in several ways. First there are three techniques supported: Calabash, Appium, and Xamarin.UITest.

Calabash is based on Cucumber, a Ruby testing framework. Therefore, the tests are written in Ruby.

Appium is a web-driver-based test framework; it was introduced to Test Cloud halfway through 2015. It supports multiple language bindings including Java, JavaScript, Python, and PHP, so you can write your tests in any of these languages.

Xamarin.UITest is based on NUnit and has full IDE support in Visual Studio and Xamarin Studio. The things you can do are the same in both frameworks, which can make the choice for one framework over the other hard. In the end, it is just a matter of taste and whatever you feel most comfortable with. In the Xamarin documentation at https://developer.xamarin.com/guides/testcloud/choosing-a-framework/, you will find a simple flowchart to help you with your decision, as shown in Figure 5-2. Appium is not shown, but where it says Calabash you could substitute Appium.

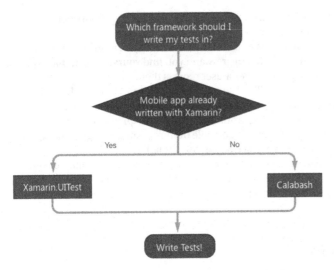

Figure 5-2. *Making a choice on the testing framework (source: Xamarin documentation)*

Basically, if your app is also a Xamarin app, you should use Xamarin.UITest. This will make it easier to start writing tests because everything will be in C#. Also, if you want to run the tests locally and not in Test Cloud, this is the choice for you.

If your app is written in Java, Objective-C/Swift, or even a hybrid app, you should choose Calabash. No special tooling is required; you can write tests in Ruby in your favorite text editor or Ruby IDE and upload the script as part of your CI builds.

For the remainder of this chapter, I will assume you are building a Xamarin app, and thus I will use the Xamarin.UITest framework. As a bonus, you can then also use the Xamarin Test Recorder. At the time of writing, this tool is in preview. It does what it sounds like: it record tests. Normally you would write the tests by hand by using Visual Studio or Xamarin Studio, and then you would spend some time on figuring out how to reach that one control. Test Recorder helps you with this. With Test Recorder, you can run your app as you normally would—on either the emulator or a physical device—and as you go through your test script, all the steps are written for you in C# code. The only thing that remains when you have recorded all the steps is to add the assertions.

There are some requirements when you want to use the Test Recorder. For more information on this, please refer to the Xamarin documentation page at https:// developer.xamarin.com/guides/testcloud/testrecorder/.

If you want to follow along with the rest of this chapter, make sure you have signed up for Test Cloud. It should be a pretty straightforward process. Just go to https://www. xamarin.com/test-cloud and either start a free trail or sign up for a plan immediately.

Creating a test consists of roughly two steps: creating a *test run*, which defines the devices and OS versions you want to run the tests on, and the *UI tests*, which are the actual test scenarios and steps that define a test.

Creating a Test Run

A suite of multiple tests is called a *test run*. To create one, log into your Test Cloud account. When you do, you will be presented with a dashboard screen, which should look like Figure 5-3.

Figure 5-3. *Test Cloud dashboard*

When you log in for the first time, you will see some sample apps. These can be helpful when exploring Test Cloud for the first time. If you want to see what is down the road, click around in them a bit. You will see how the test results are presented and what the possibilities are without having to upload your own app.

Whenever you are ready, click the New Test Run button in the top bar. In the screen that pops up, you have to choose whether you will be creating an Android or iOS test run. When you have decided, you will be taken to the next screen where you get to choose the devices that you want the tests to run on. For this example, I have chosen the iOS path, but I assure you the Android process is the same, except for the devices you get to pick.

The list of devices is actually easy to work with. You can sort it by the following:

- *Estimated wait time*: Since Test Cloud works with physical devices, there is only a limited number of devices available. As the number of users is growing, there will be some waiting before your test can commence if the device of your choosing turns out to be a popular pick. With this option, you can select the devices that have a short queue time.

- *Availability*: With this option, you sort the devices by how generally available they are. The more people who own a device, the higher it will be on the list. This way you can easily target the most popular devices.

- *Name*: This one should be self-explanatory; it just arranges the list of devices from *A* to *Z*.

- *OS version*: When you choose this option, you will rearrange the list by version of the OS, with the newest first. Note that prereleases are not supported. Only versions that have been released to the public are available. So, you cannot use Test Cloud to test your app on prerelease versions.

Figure 5-4 shows the screen where you can select and sort devices.

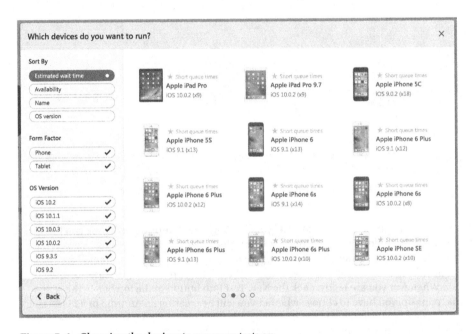

Figure 5-4. *Choosing the devices to run your tests on*

In addition to sorting, you can filter the list of devices. Check or uncheck a specific form factor or hide certain OS versions or hardware.

Whenever you see a device that you want to include in the test cycle, simply click it and then click the next one to select that one as well. Select at least one device to proceed. There is no upper limit; I have tried selecting more than 100 devices and Test Cloud continued without any problems. Just remember your device hours and concurrency. This means if you write a test that takes 1 minute, you will be able to run it on a maximum of 60 devices each day on the first tier, and thus you never can run your test on all 100 devices.

Whenever you are happy with your selection, click the Next button, which takes you to a screen where you need to configure the last part. Here you can connect this test run to a certain *series* with which you can basically divide your test runs into a category. You can then not only trigger a certain test run but also a series that can contain multiple test runs.

The other thing you can configure here is which system language your selected devices should have. Before the test run commences, the devices' language will be set to the one you have set here.

From there you go to the last screen. While you would expect at this step something gets saved into your Test Cloud account, that is not the case. Instead, you will be presented with some command-line commands, as shown in Figure 5-5.

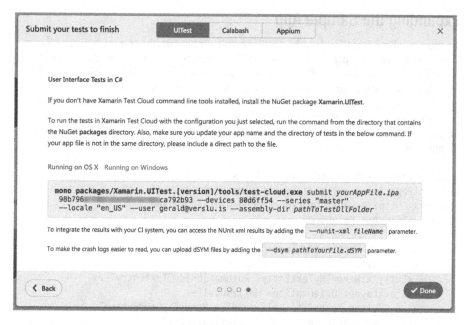

Figure 5-5. *Final screen of creating a test run*

So, when you reach this screen, do not just click the Done button because you will have to go through the whole procedure again. Instead, copy the whole command to somewhere for later use.

If you look at it closely, you can figure out all the different ingredients that you have used before. Most importantly, there is the devices switch: --devices 80d6ff54. This hash resembles the device configurations that you have selected, and this is the one you need later in order to specify on which devices you will run your tests.

The other important thing here is the hash after yourAppFile.ipa, which is obscured in Figure 5-5. This is your API key. You will need this later.

With all this in place, you now have everything to start writing actual tests, which is what you will do in the next section.

Creating a App UI Test

Before I will show you how you can create UI tests with the Xamarin.UITest framework, I will expand my CiCdApp a little bit so that there is something to test. If you are not interested in how the testing applies to my sample project but rather would like to link it to your own, you can skip the next section and go right to "Write Your Tests."

Expanding the Sample App

To show you how Test Cloud works, I will create a simple interface for my app so you can look at the basic concepts. For my app, I will be using Xamarin.Forms, but most of the procedures should be identical. I will try to point out where the process differs and why.

Up until now my app was not much more than an empty shell to demonstrate continuous integration and building. To show you how creating tests work, I will add a little bit more body to my application. In the MainPage.xaml file, I will add one text box and two buttons; one button will add some text into the text box, the other button will not do anything. In XAML, it will look like the following:

```xml
<?xml version="1.0" encoding="utf-8" ?>
<ContentPage xmlns="http://xamarin.com/schemas/2014/forms"
 xmlns:x="http://schemas.microsoft.com/winfx/2009/xaml"
 x:Class="CiCdApp.MainPage">

    <StackLayout VerticalOptions="CenterAndExpand"
      HorizontalOptions="CenterAndExpand">
        <Entry x:Name="MyTextEntry" AutomationId="TextEntry" />
        <StackLayout Orientation="Horizontal">
            <Button Text="It's all good" x:Name="MyGoodButton"
              AutomationId="GoodButtonForTextEntry"
              Clicked="MyGoodButton_OnClicked" TextColor="Green" />
            <Button Text="BOOM" x:Name="MyBadButton"
              AutomationId="BadButtonForTextEntry" TextColor="Red" />
        </StackLayout>
    </StackLayout>
</ContentPage>
```

Notice how I have given all the controls a name, but also I have specified the AutomationId attribute. This attribute was introduced with Xamarin.Forms 2.2.0; before that, the StyleId property was commonly (mis)used. The purpose of this property is to easily identify a control and access it within your tests. You will learn how you do this in the next paragraph.

This piece of XAML results in the interface shown in Figure 5-6. Here you see the output with a green button and a red button under a text box. The green button represents a successful test; the red button represents a failing one. Of course, since the app is built with Xamarin Forms, the Android and UWP projects will show similar output.

Figure 5-6. *The expanded sample app*

Also, notice the event handler attached to the green button. This has some basic code to set the value of the text box, like so:

```
private void MyGoodButton_OnClicked(object sender, EventArgs e)
{
        MyTextEntry.Text = "TADA!";
}
```

Handling events and referencing controls from the code-behind is not a best practice and should be avoided in favor of testability and reusability, but since we are not focusing on the actual tests here, this will suffice for this example.

The other (red) button will *should* enter a text in the input field, but we do not implement this functionality on purpose to create a failing test.

This concludes the expansion of my sample app so I can show you the basics of writing a UI test for Test Cloud, which you will do in the next section.

Write Your Tests

There are a few things I need to cover before you can run your tests. The first step applies only to your iOS project; install the Xamarin.TestCloud.Agent NuGet package. To make sure the Calabash library is initialized, also go into your AppDelegate.cs file and add this piece of code:

```
#if ENABLE_TEST_CLOUD
Xamarin.Calabash.Start();
#endif
```

The position does not matter; I tend to add it at the beginning. If you are a more experienced developer, you probably know what this does. With a compiler directive, you specify that this piece of code will be included only if the ENABLE_TEST_CLOUD constant value is in your project's current configuration properties. If you are using Visual Studio, this means whenever you switch the build configuration (i.e., to Debug or AppStore), you will see this piece of code light up when the constant is defined in your project properties for this configuration.

■ **Note**   Make sure the ENABLE_TEST_CLOUD compiler directive is not enabled in the build configuration that you use to create an App Store build. The Test Cloud Calabash libraries use some private Apple APIs, which will not pass the App Store review process.

To see which constants are defined, go to your iOS project, right-click, and choose Properties. On the Build tab, you will find what you are looking for. Figure 5-7 shows this tab with the current constant values.

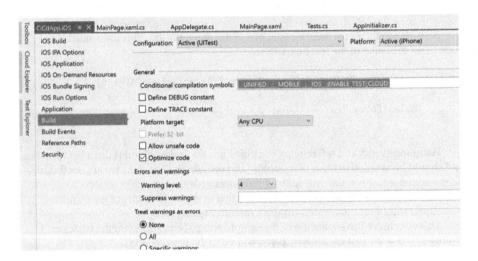

Figure 5-7. *Build tab of the iOS project*

In the "Conditional compilation symbols" box, you can define your own symbols. In newer versions of Xamarin Studio and Visual Studio, the Test Cloud flag should already be there. With this, you can include (or exclude) certain pieces of code based on a certain build configuration. People can debate whether this is a good way to do this, but personally I do not think so; however, for this kind of use case, it is useful.

As you can see in Figure 5-7 I have created a separate configuration for the UI tests. This configuration has the ENABLE_TEST_CLOUD flag, and thus the Calabash library is linked and executed. You will learn more about using this in the next chapter.

While you are in the iOS project properties, go to the iOS IPA Options tab and make sure the check box "Build ad-hoc/enterprise (IPA)" is selected. This will build an actual .ipa file. This is the executable file for iOS devices, which you will need to run your tests with.

After completing this, you can add the actual test project to your solution. Right-click your solution, click Add, and choose New Project. See Figure 5-8, which shows the new project screen. You can find the UI Test App template under multiple categories; they are all the same. The most obvious place is Test. If you look at the other options here, you can see test projects for unit tests as well as UI test projects specifically for iOS and Android. My sample CiCdApp, however, is a Xamarin.Forms app, so I will choose the cross-platform one. Writing tests should not be any different; only the selection of (UI) controls will be a bit different, as you will see in a little bit.

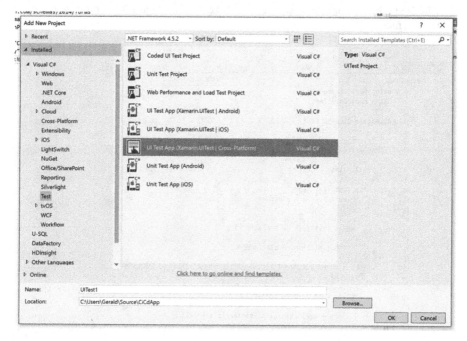

Figure 5-8. *Adding the UI Test App project to your solution*

After naming and adding the new test project to your solution, you see it pop up in the Solution Explorer in Visual Studio. It consists of two files: AppInitializer.cs and Tests.cs. As you may expect, these files contain global app configurations and concrete test cases, respectively.

Before getting into these files, there is one thing you need to do to prepare your test project, and that is to reference your app projects. In the newly created test project, click the References node and then choose Add Reference. In the screen that comes up, check the iOS and/or Droid project and close it with the OK button.

In the `AppInitializer.cs` file you can tweak the configuration of the overall test app. This includes enabling the local screenshot functionality, taking screenshots when running a test locally, configuring an IP address for your device, and interacting with other apps on the device. The default configuration will do fine for now; this just does the basic configuration based on the platform you are running the tests for.

■ **Tip** Taking screenshots increases your device time a bit, which can start to add up as your tests grow. You can declare a global variable with which you can easily enable or disable the screenshot functionality.

The `Tests.cs` file contains concrete tests. Take a look at Figure 5-9 for the generated code in this file.

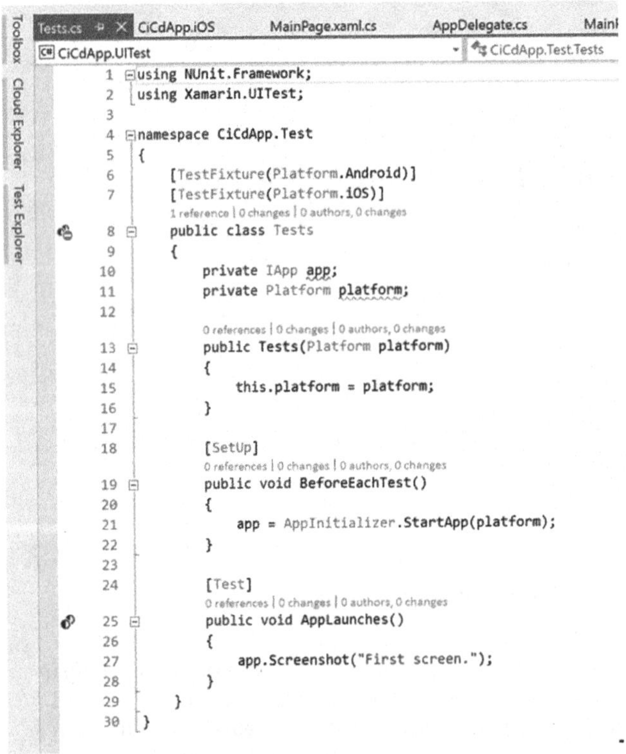

```csharp
using NUnit.Framework;
using Xamarin.UITest;

namespace CiCdApp.Test
{
    [TestFixture(Platform.Android)]
    [TestFixture(Platform.iOS)]
    public class Tests
    {
        private IApp app;
        private Platform platform;

        public Tests(Platform platform)
        {
            this.platform = platform;
        }

        [SetUp]
        public void BeforeEachTest()
        {
            app = AppInitializer.StartApp(platform);
        }

        [Test]
        public void AppLaunches()
        {
            app.Screenshot("First screen.");
        }
    }
}
```

Figure 5-9. Default generated test code

A few things should stand out. Let's start from the top. Above the class declaration you see two `TestFixture` attributes. A test fixture is a group of tests (it can also be just one) that logically fit together. What *logical* means is up to you. You could group them by platform, type of functionality, and so on. To do this, just create a new class, give the class a name you can easily identify it with, and apply a new `TextFixture` attribute with a value you can identify this set of tests with.

If you look a bit further to the other attributes, you see `SetUp` and `Test` attributes above two methods within the class. The `SetUp` attribute denotes a method that will be run before each test method. With the default code shown in Figure 5-9 before each test, the `IApp` instance is initialized again. This happens so that values and states remembered in that instance do not influence other tests. If there is any other code that should be initialized before each separate test, put it here.

The `IApp` instance contains all kinds of ways to interact with the UI. With this object, you can simulate tapping controls, swiping, scrolling up and down, and much more. The instance also provides access to information about the device and gives you the ability to print something to the logs.

■ **Note**   The `IApp` instance does *not* mean the actual running app. The running app will remain the same. For instance, when you look at the CiCdApp sample when you click the button, the text will stay in the text box until it is cleared. The app will not be restarted or cleared in between the different tests.

Each method that is marked with the `Test` attribute is a test run. One method will translate to one test in Test Cloud. For the test methods, the Arrange-Act-Assert pattern is advised. If you have worked with testing before, this will sound familiar.

There are not any real technical implications; this is just a way of writing your tests. You first write some code, which is needed as preparation for this specific test; then you *arrange* everything for your test case. The next step is to do the actual calls for your test, so you *act*. Here you execute the actual logic.

Finally, you match the actual results with the results you are expecting, which is where you *assert* the outcome. With one or more assertions, you check each condition, for example, whether the value in the text box changed, whether the user navigated to the next page, and so on.

This is the pattern I will be using in the upcoming tests. For clarity I will distinguish the three sections by comments in each test method. This is something I tend to do in real life as well to increase readability for the next developer who looks at these tests.

Let's take a look at writing some simple tests. I will enrich the Tests.cs file with some extra tests, which you can find here:

```
[Test]
public void AppLaunches()
{
    // Not a real test, just here to have some first reference
    app.Screenshot("First screen.");
}

[Test]
public void Press_Good_Button_And_Pass_Hooray()
{
    // Arrange
    // Nothing to arrange for this test

    // Act
    app.Tap(e => e.Marked("GoodButtonForTextEntry"));
    app.Screenshot("Test TADA! entered");

    // Assert
    Assert.AreEqual("TADA!", app.Query(e =>
        e.Marked("TextEntry")).First().Text);
}

[Test]
public void Press_Bad_Button_And_Fail_Boo()
{
    // Arrange
    app.ClearText("TextEntry");

    // Act
    app.Tap(e => e.Marked("BadButtonForTextEntry"));
    app.Screenshot("Text should not be entered");

    Assert.AreEqual("TADA!", app.Query(e =>
        e.Marked("TextEntry")).First().Text);
}
```

In this code snippet I have shown only the test methods; the rest of the code in that class has not been changed. I will cover the test methods briefly; they should be pretty straightforward.

The AppLaunches test is just there to provide a starting point. You will receive a screenshot of the first screen, and that is it. If that does not fail with any exceptions, the test will pass.

There are two other tests here, and the method names describe what the test does and what result is expected. Although in this case they could be more descriptive, this is a common thing to do when writing tests. The Press_Good_Button_And_Pass_Hooray method is already modeled with the Arrange-Act-Assert pattern. Since there is nothing specific to arrange, you can skip that and go right to acting. In this case, you should find the green button and tap it. This is done with this line: app.Tap(e => e.Marked("Good ButtonForTextEntry");. As mentioned earlier, you know that the app variable holds an instance of the IApp object and can be used for interactions with your controls. Inside the Tap method, you can see a lambda expression to find the right control. While you can locate controls in any way you want, I find the easiest way is to use the AutomationId I have specified with all my controls. If you have set the AutomationId property, you can find it with the Marked method, or you can even leave the Marked method out and use the shorthand app.Tap("GoodButtonForTextEntry");. After it is tapped, you can take another screenshot so you can verify the outcome visually. The final step is to assert.

The Assert object is a static object that has all kinds of functions to compare values. In this case, with the line Assert.AreEqual("TADA!", app.Query(e => e.Marked("TextEntry")).First().Text); you check your expected value (TADA!) against the actual value in the text box. You obtain a reference to this control, again with its AutomationId value (in this case TextEntry), and just get the value out of the Text property. If they are equal, the test will succeed. My last test, called Press_Bad_Button_ And_Fail_Boo, basically does the same thing; however, the button will not enter any text in the text box. Since you do expect it to according to the assert statement, you know beforehand this test will fail.

Before you send these tests to Test Cloud for processing, there is one more important thing to note. The AutomationId property I have been using a lot now is a very Xamarin. Forms-specific concept. Traditional Xamarin projects do not enrich the controls available with AutomationId, and this attribute by itself does nothing, not even in Xamarin.Forms. Remember, all that Forms does is "translate" abstract controls to the native controls on that platform.

Because of this, you must pass the value you use to identify a control, which you keep in the AutomationId property, to a property in the native control as well. This should be a property that is available in all controls. For iOS, the best choice is AccessibilityIdentifier; for Android it's ContentDescription. At this time, Xamarin does not make this translation for you, and maybe it never will in order to keep it flexible and a choice for you to make. However, Xamarin has defined these two native control properties as the equivalents of the AutomationId property. Because of that, the Marked method to identify a control looks at these native properties.

To get the values into the right native properties, you must add some extra code to your apps.

For iOS, go into your AppDelegate.cs file and find the FinishedLaunching method. This is the method where you also added the Test Cloud initialization code. At this point, add the following piece of code after the Forms.Init(); line:

```
Forms.ViewInitialized += (object sender, ViewInitializedEventArgs e) => {
    if (!string.IsNullOrWhiteSpace(e.View.AutomationId))
    {
        e.NativeView.AccessibilityIdentifier = e.View.AutomationId;
    }
};
```

This hooks into the event handler on a very high level, triggering whenever a View object is initialized. When that happens, you set the iOS native property AccessibilityIdentifier to the value of AutomationId in your Forms control. Depending on how complex your UI is, you might want to wrap this in the ENABLE_TEST_CLOUD compiler directive so it is executed only whenever you create a Test Cloud build.

Something similar is needed for Android. Here you go to the MainActivity.cs file again, and in the OnCreate method you add the following piece of code, also after the Forms.Init() method:

```
Xamarin.Forms.Forms.ViewInitialized += (object sender, Xamarin.Forms.
ViewInitializedEventArgs e) => {
    if (!string.IsNullOrWhiteSpace(e.View.AutomationId))
    {
        e.NativeView.ContentDescription = e.View.AutomationId;
    }
};
```

If you are not using Forms but building an app with traditional Xamarin, you can just go ahead and fill the AccessibilityIdentifier and ContentDescription properties directly.

With what you have learned, you now know all the basics to go and write your own tests! I could elaborate a lot more on all the methods that are available or sum up all the best practices, but that is enough material to fill a book on its own. Since I am focusing on CI and CD, I will not handle all of it here. I do hope that I have shown you how easy testing is to set up and how powerful tests can be. If you want to dive into the topic deeper, a good starting point is the Xamarin documentation at https://developer.xamarin.com/guides/testcloud/introduction-to-test-cloud/.

■ **Tip**   Earlier I mentioned the Test Recorder application. This application can help you write your UI tests a lot quicker. Test Recorder runs alongside your emulator or physical device and turns all the interactions you do with your app into UI test code. The only thing that remains is to add the arrange and asserts to complete your test cases. Since you only have to click through your app, you can even have your tester do it!

Running Your Tests in Test Cloud

Now that you have some tests, let's see if they work!

As you may recall, there are two different ways you can run the tests: locally on an emulator or physical device or by sending them to Test Cloud. When you run tests locally, it goes without saying that they will not eat into your device hours, and you can run them as much and as long as you like. But, if you run them on an emulator, this will not necessarily represent a physical device. While you can incorporate your devices you have lying around in your building pipeline, this is probably not something you want. If you did that, you would have to maintain the device, install updates, and make sure it still works from time to time—all stuff that you do not want to be bothered with.

I will be focusing on running the tests on Test Cloud. There are a few ways of uploading your tests. In the remainder of this chapter, I will cover how to upload a test manually and look at the results. In the next chapter, you will learn how to integrate these tests as part of your automated builds.

The first way to upload is through the command line. Remember the command that you got presented with on the Test Cloud dashboard when you were creating a test run? That is the command you can use now. Find the test-cloud.exe executable in the packages folder of your solution and gather your app's .ipa and/or .apk file and the folder that contains your test DLL. Then invoke the command you saved earlier in a terminal window. This can be done from either Windows or Mac. In Figure 5-10 you will see what it looks like to upload and run tests in a terminal window on the Mac.

Figure 5-10. Uploading the tests through the command line

Besides the options that are shown in Figure 5-10, there are a couple more you can use to influence the process. For instance, you can run only a specific category. To get help for this tool, just type mono test-cloud.exe help.

Right after uploading the test, it will be run on Test Cloud. If you were to go into the dashboard now, you would see your test show up there.

Another way of doing this is through the IDE. Both Visual Studio and Xamarin Studio have options in the context menu of the testing project to send all the needed files to Test Cloud. Under the hood it executes these commands for you, but it looks a bit more user-friendly.

After examining the output in the console window for a while, the status should change to something that states your tests are being executed. When you now go to the Test Cloud dashboard, you will see your app show up, and when you click it, the test runs for this app. In Figure 5-11 you can see how the test is being executed right now.

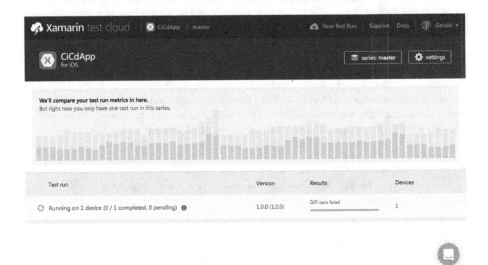

Figure 5-11. *Test being executed on Test Cloud*

After a few test runs, you will see a summary of all the results. Test Cloud will show you how many tests are executed each run, how many passed or failed, what the app size was, and how much memory was used.

When the test is complete, it will show up in this screen; also, the results will be visible in the terminal window. Click the test to view the detailed results for this run. Figure 5-12 shows the screen.

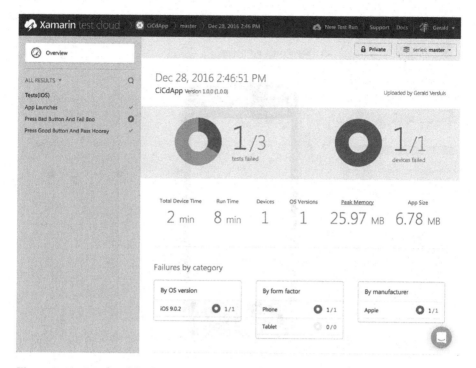

Figure 5-12. *Results of the first test run*

In this screen on the left, you see all the different tests that you have defined in your test fixture. I will get back to those in just a second. The right part of the screen shows an overview of this run. There are convenient diagrams and numbers that sum up how it went. In this case, you see that one test out of the three have failed, and thus one out of one device failed. Right underneath you see how much device time you have used up on how many devices, and so on.

Below that, there is some more data that is categorized by OS, form factor, and other criteria.

On the left, you see the different tests. You can see the method names that you gave them, and Test Cloud even replaced the underscores with spaces for readability. You can also see in one glimpse which of these tests failed. When you click one of the tests, you will see all the steps that are taken in this test.

When you click the failed test, you will see the test device appear on the right along with some technical details about it. Take a look at Figure 5-13, which shows this screen.

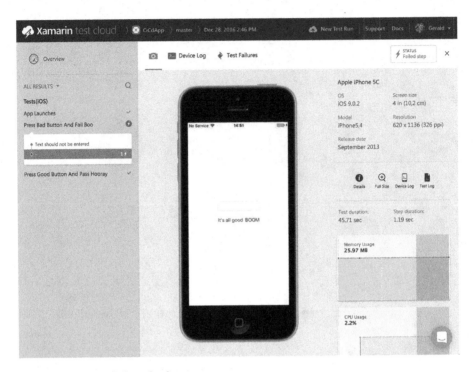

Figure 5-13. *Detailed result of a test*

To diagnose what exactly went wrong, you can go to the Test Failures tab. This shows the outcome of the assert statement, in this case: "Expected string length 5 but was 0. Strings differ at index 0. Expected: "TADA!" But was: <string.Empty>." So, now you know what went wrong, or maybe what went right with a wrong test.

If you need to examine in more detail what seems to be going wrong, you can also go into the device or test log.

Whenever you have multiple devices selected for this test run, you will see all the selected devices on the right side along with a red icon on the top right to indicate whether that test failed on that specific device. You could then zoom in to the view, which is shown in Figure 5-13.

In this chapter, you saw how to write tests and run them on Test Cloud. I hope you get to play with Test Cloud for a bit and you get as enthusiastic about it as I am. You will soon find out how powerful it is. I distinctively remember one of the first test cases I wrote. It was a single page with a button near the bottom of the page. At the time, I had an iPhone 6, and it all worked perfectly and looked nice. I decided to write some tests for it to see how it would act on other devices and form factors. For my test run, I selected a variety of devices ranging from iPhone 4 devices up to iPhone 6 Plus devices. It was such a simple screen that I did not expect much from it. To my big surprise, on some devices it failed!

Upon inspection, it turned out that the test failed on devices with a smaller form factor, and I looked into what went wrong according to the logs. It said something along the lines of "Unable to tap element." Time to look at the screenshots! I noticed that the button on the bottom was not visible. Curious as to what was going on, I fired up the project on a simulator and immediately noticed what was wrong. I forgot to add a scroll to it, so on smaller form factor devices the user was not able to reach the button. Hence, the app could not be interacted with, and I would have never noticed without these tests.

If you think about this for a second, this is really powerful. I wrote the tests for interacting with my app in code, and in code the control could be found. But the tests and Test Cloud simulate interactions so well that they also notice when something is off-screen and cannot be reached by a real-life user.

Final Thoughts

I hope you are as enthusiastic about Xamarin Test Cloud as I am. This is really a unique service. With a (relatively) small investment, you are able to test your app on devices that you did not even know existed. You will get a grip on regression within your code and locate bugs on specific devices with different operating system combinations. The best part is that it is not solely for Xamarin apps!

In this chapter, you learned what Test Cloud is and how you can start writing tests for it. You learned how to upload your app to Test Cloud and run a test on it. While this is working great, your goal is to automate as much as possible. That is what you will be looking at in the next chapter, where you will see how you can run tests as an integral part of your build.

CHAPTER 6

Integrating Tests into Your Builds

In the previous chapter, you learned how to add a test project to your solution, write UI tests, and run them in Test Cloud. While this is a great step forward already, ideally you want to have tests run as part of your automated build pipeline. By adding the instructions to your build definitions, you can benefit even more because you do not have to worry about running the tests yourself. The results will be presented to you automatically.

This chapter will cover how to integrate triggering tests into your continuous integration. Maybe even more important, you'll learn how you can aggregate the results so you can collect feedback as early as possible. Specifically, you will learn how to integrate the Test Cloud tests that you created in the previous chapter. Also, you will look at how you can create some simple unit tests to go along with them and run those as well.

Integrating Test Cloud as Part of Continuous Integration

To show you how to integrate Test Cloud, I will continue to use my CiCdApp project as an example. I have committed all the code that I created in the previous chapter, so it is available in the repository.

Go to VSTS and take a look at the build definitions you have created so far. As you may recall from Chapter 3, there were already steps in your build definition to run Test Cloud tests, but you disabled them for the time being. Go into the iOS build definition and find the Test Cloud step. When you take a closer look at the configuration on the right side of the screen, you will suddenly see a lot of familiar fields. Figure 6-1 shows the screen with this configuration.

© Gerald Versluis 2017
G. Versluis, *Xamarin Continuous Integration and Delivery*,
DOI 10.1007/978-1-4842-2716-9_6

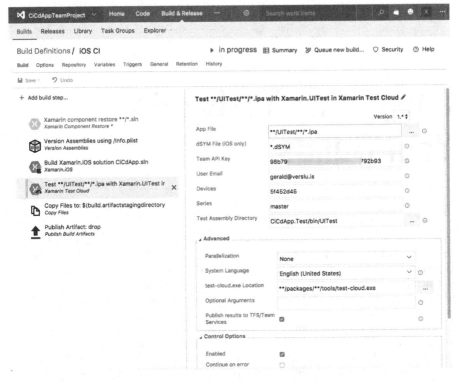

Figure 6-1. Configuration of the Test Cloud task

Let's go through all the fields from top to bottom.

- *App File*: The binaries are your app, so this setting is your `.apk` or `.ipa` file for Android and iOS, respectively. You can work with the minimatch pattern and select multiple files this way. Note that for each binary that is found, a test run will be fired. So, make sure only one is submitted so it will not eat up precious device time. For example, you can do this by cleaning your build folder before you start.

■ **Tip**   If you are looking for an easy way to clean your folders before a build, go to the Repository tab and select the Clean option. You will be able to configure whether the folder should be cleaned and whether the source and output folders should be cleaned.

- *dSYM File*: This is only for iOS applications. Building an `.ipa` binary also results in a `.dSYM` file containing the debug symbols. With this file, more informative stack traces can be generated when your application crashes. Although it is not necessary to provide this file, it can be helpful to do so.

- *Team API Key*: This is the API key that you are identified with at Test Cloud. Together with your e-mail, this is your user name and password combination.

- *User Email*: As mentioned, this is your user name and the account that you log in with on the Test Cloud dashboard.

- *Devices*: As you may recall from Chapter 5, there was a hash generated for the devices you selected to run your tests on. This field is where you enter that hash.

- *Series*: In Test Cloud, you could have created different test series. If you want to run a specific series, this is where you can configure it. For now, leave it at the default value.

- *Test Assembly Directory*: This is the directory in which the assemblies reside that contain the tests. This will be the output folder of your test project.

As you might have noticed, these values correspond with the command-line parameters you got from Test Cloud when you were constructing your test run. Fill in the right values in this task and save it.

Under these basic configuration fields there are some more in the Advanced section. You can leave these settings at their default values for now. The most notable is the check box at the bottom: "Publish results to TFS/Team Services." By selecting this box, you retrieve the results from Test Cloud and embed them right here in VSTS. You will see what that looks like a little later in this chapter.

If you have created a separate build configuration, you need to change that on the Variables tab. In my case, I will set the BuildConfiguration value to UITest.

■ **Note** While I will now incorporate the Test Cloud task into my CI build, this may not be what is right for you. When your tests start to grow and the running time increases, you might want to create a separate definition to send your app to Test Cloud. Maybe even more important, the CI build is ideally triggered with each (small) change in your code. When you send each change through Test Cloud, your device hours might run out fast. For brevity, I just incorporate running tests in Test Cloud into my existing build definition.

After saving all the changes, it is time to see whether everything is configured correctly. Trigger a build with the "Queue new build..." button and sit back to watch what happens. When the build is triggered and the log window comes up, examine the part where the Test Cloud step is executed. Look at Figure 6-2 for the output of my build.

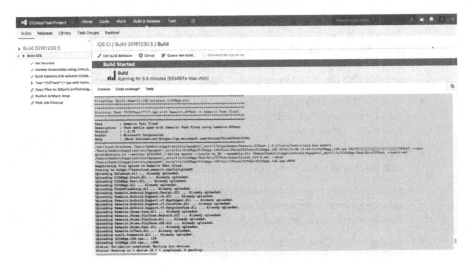

Figure 6-2. *Log output from Test Cloud*

When you look closely, you will notice that the output is the same as the output from your command-line upload process. The explanation for this is simple: the same tool is being used by VSTS.

■ **Tip** One error that is likely to occur here is this: "The `.ipa` file does not seem to be linked with Calabash framework." This is referring to the code to initialize the Calabash framework, so the code in your `ENABLE_TEST_CLOUD` compiler directive has not been executed. Make sure you ran the right build configuration and that you are uploading the right `.ipa` file.

After the test has finished, wait for the rest of the build to complete to inspect the outcome.

Since I did not fix my test, you can expect the same result as earlier: two tests will pass, and one will fail. This is exactly what happened when running this build.

Also, I left the check box on to gather the test results in VSTS, so let's take a look at that. Figure 6-3 shows how these results are visualized.

Figure 6-3. *Summary of the gathered results from Test Cloud*

What is really great about having the test results gathered is that you can see what went wrong right in VSTS. There is a summary of all tests, and you can see in one glance how many tests succeeded and how many failed, how much time they took, and some more data around that. If you also have unit tests or any other tests that can report their results to VSTS, the results are aggregated here. This enables you to gather all information about the quality of your app right here from one dashboard.

When you click a specific test, you will be presented with the results for that test. As you saw in the previous chapter, there was an error message with the failing test. This same message is presented to you, but this time within VSTS.

The only thing lacking in VSTS is the ability to look at the screenshots that are taken or the details per device. There are some VSTS extensions in the marketplace that provide you with these, and the integration probably will be implemented in the future.

■ **Tip**   If you want your build not to fail but to be set to Partially Succeeded when one or more tests fail, go to your build definition and Test Cloud task and select the check box "Continue on error."

Integrating Unit Tests

Like every good developer, you have, of course, numerous unit tests in your projects as well. (Right?) You can easily run these as an integral part of your builds. No special extensions are needed for this; the ability is already built into VSTS. At least, it is when you use the MSTest, NUnit, or xUnit engine to create and run your tests. All of these are supported in VSTS and popular for various reasons.

To get you on the right path, let's take a quick look at how to create some simple unit tests and integrate them into your builds.

There are multiple sorts of unit tests that you can incorporate in respect to Xamarin apps. If you are using Xamarin.Forms (or even if you are not but you do have a shared code base library), you can use a "normal" unit test project.

For traditional Xamarin apps or if there is some platform-specific code that you need to test, there are special unit tests projects for each platform. I will quickly go over all the options together and show a small example for each scenario.

Unit Testing Shared Code

First let's take a look at writing tests for the shared code. To have something to test, I have added another page to CiCdApp, but more importantly I have added a page model. If you are familiar with the Model-View-ViewModel (MVVM) pattern, you will know that each page has a corresponding page model that contains all the properties and logic for a certain view.

The page and page model I have added to my Portable Class Library (PCL) project are named CalculatorPage and CalculatorPageModel. They will contain simple logic to add and multiply two numbers, as well as giving you the answer to life, the universe, and everything. Since these are unit tests and not UI tests, I will be focusing on the page model.

Before discussing the code that I have created for this, I will zoom in a bit on the PCL project I just mentioned. If you have developed Xamarin apps before, you might have heard about so-called shared projects and PCL projects. These types of projects are the ways to share code for Xamarin apps. Describing the differences in detail would be beyond the scope of this book, but for clarity I will briefly describe the basics.

A PCL project will compile into a DLL file, while a shared project is nothing more than a folder with code that is shared between the platform projects. When compiling the code in a shared project, the code will become part of the platform project and is an integral part of the assembly.

The Portable Class Library was a first attempt by Microsoft to create a cross-platform library with which you can share code. For a while it was only cross-platform between Microsoft platforms, but with the support in Xamarin, it became more popular because it now actually supports multiple platforms. In time, .NET Standard Libraries will probably replace the PCL or at least become more popular.

The biggest difference between the two lies in the support for features of the .NET framework. With shared projects, you have access to all features of the .NET framework. You can differentiate code for the separate platforms with *compiler directives*. In a PCL project, you specify the platforms that you want to support, and the features of the .NET framework that are available to you are dependent on that selection. You will get support only for the functionality that is available on each platform that you want to support. Of course, there are ways to implement platform-specific code for PCL projects as well.

Each solution has its pros and cons, and basically it comes down to a matter of taste because both solutions achieve the same result. I personally tend to like the PCL projects. The code is more separated and is easier to reuse. It just feels cleaner.

■ **Tip** For more information on ways to share code and the details on Shared projects and PCLs, please refer to the Xamarin developer documentation on this subject: `https://developer.xamarin.com/guides/cross-platform/application_fundamentals/code-sharing/`.

Now that you have learned about what a PCL is, let's take a look at the page model I have added. The implementation looks like this:

```
public class CalculatorPageModel
{
    public ICommand AddCommand { get; private set; }
    public ICommand MultiplyCommand { get; private set; }
    public ICommand AnswerToEverythingCommand { get; private set; }

    public int ValueA { get; set; }
    public int ValueB { get; set; }
    public int Result { get; set; }

    public CalculatorPageModel()
    {
        AddCommand = new Command(Add);
        MultiplyCommand = new Command(Multiply);
        AnswerToEverythingCommand = new Command(AnswerToEverything);
    }

    private void Add()
    {
        Result = ValueA + ValueB;
    }

    private void Multiply()
    {
        Result = ValueA * ValueB;
    }
```

```
private void AnswerToEverything()
{
    Result = 1337;
}
}
```

As you can see, there is nothing exciting going on here, but it gives you some code to write tests for.

Now you just add a regular unit test project to your solution. In Figure 6-4 you can see the Add New Project screen where you can select the Unit Test Project template.

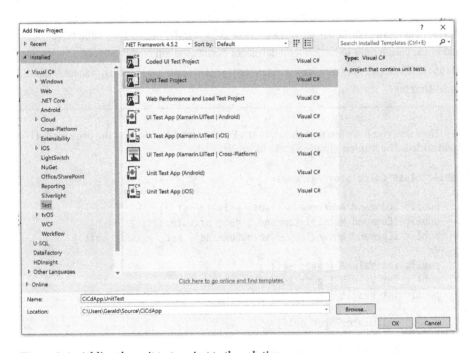

Figure 6-4. *Adding the unit test project to the solution*

After Visual Studio does some generating, you will have a bare setup of a unit test fixture in the UnitTests1.cs file. If you look a bit closer, you will notice the structure is much like the Test Cloud test structure. The naming convention on the attributes is a bit different, but the way you write tests is the same.

In the following code block, you will see how I defined test cases for my methods in the page model:

```
[TestClass]
public class CalculatorUnitTests
{
    private CalculatorPageModel _pageModel;
```

```
[TestInitialize]
public void Initialize()
{
    _pageModel = new CalculatorPageModel();
}

[TestMethod]
public void AddTest()
{
    // Arrange
    _pageModel.ValueA = 20;
    _pageModel.ValueB = 22;

    // Act
    _pageModel.AddCommand.Execute(null);

    // Assert
    Assert.AreEqual(42, _pageModel.Result);
}

[TestMethod]
public void MultiplyTest()
{
    // Arrange
    _pageModel.ValueA = 6;
    _pageModel.ValueB = 7;

    // Act
    _pageModel.MultiplyCommand.Execute(null);

    // Assert
    Assert.AreEqual(42, _pageModel.Result);
}

[TestMethod]
public void AnswerToEverythingTest()
{
    // Arrange
    // Nothing to arrange for this test

    // Act
    _pageModel.AnswerToEverythingCommand.Execute(null);

    // Assert
    Assert.AreEqual(42, _pageModel.Result);
}
}
```

As I just mentioned, there are a few different terms here: `TestFixture` is now a `TestClass`, `SetUp` is now a `TestInitialize`, and `Test` is now a `TestMethod`. Other than that, the concepts are the same. You will notice that in the initializer method I create a reference to the page model. This method—just like the method marked with the `SetUp` attribute in the UI tests—will be executed before each test. This way, you get a fresh state of the page model so one test does not influence the other. Also, just like the UI tests, you can follow the Act-Arrange-Assert pattern for the unit tests as well.

The body of the test methods should be pretty straightforward. However, I did make a mistake. In the page model, I return the number 1337 as the answer to life, the universe, and everything, but of course this should be 42. (Obviously!) So, you will know this test will fail. The other tests should pass.

When you right-click the unit test project, there is the option Run Unit Tests to run all the tests in the project; you can also do this per class or even per test method. When you run them, the projects will be built, and the Unit Test Sessions screen will pop up showing you the progress of the selected tests. Figure 6-5 shows you the output of the tests I have created.

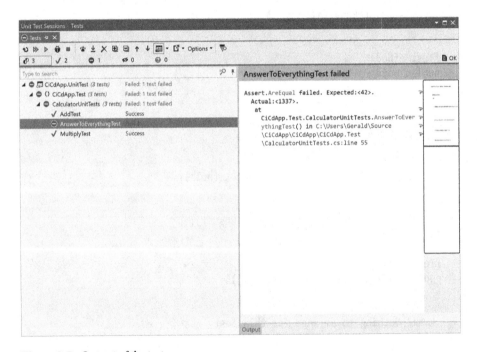

Figure 6-5. *Output of the test run*

As expected, one test failed, and it tells you exactly why. I will not fix it now, so you can see the output in VSTS as well. As your test cases are becoming more complex, you might want to debug it to see whether your test is wrong or your code is wrong. In the same context menu where you first started these tests there is also the option Debug Unit Tests. With these options you can set breakpoints like you regularly would and step through your code, analyzing what is going wrong.

The true power of your test lies with running them in an automated and continuous fashion. Because unit tests should be small and can execute within seconds, they can and should be part of your continuous integration build. This way, you receive feedback about the quality of your code as soon as possible.

To achieve this, just go to your build definition and add a new step. Find the Visual Studio Test step and add it to your definition. You should add this after your main project or solution has been built since the tests cannot be run when the project does not build at all.

There are some options for you to configure, but with the default configuration you should be able to get started.

In Figure 6-6 you see the added step and configuration. There are two things that should be noted in the configuration. The first thing is the value in the first field, Test Assembly. With this field, you specify the assembly or assemblies in which your tests are. You can work with minimatch patterns to locate them. By default, VSTS should pick up all assemblies with test in them, excluding the ones under the obj folder. As you might remember from the previous chapter, the Test Cloud assemblies also have test in them, so make sure you exclude them as unit tests. That is why it's a good idea to name your projects differently so you can distinguish them by name.

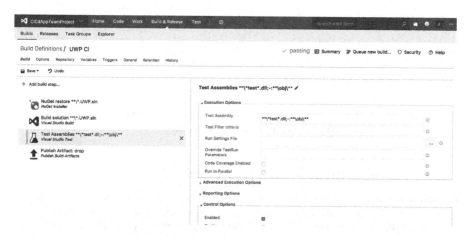

Figure 6-6. *Adding unit tests to your build definition*

The second thing you might want to do is select the Code Coverage Enabled check box. With this enabled, it will also collect data about the code coverage. This means it will tell you how much of your code is tested by the unit tests that are found; the closer you get to 100 percent, the better. As you may recall from the UI tests, you can select the "Continue on error" box here as well to not fail your build when one or more tests fail but rather have the build marked as Partially Succeeded.

All results, including the data on the code coverage, are consolidated in the results of a build, right in VSTS, just like you saw with the UI tests. Looking at Figure 6-7, you see a similar screen with tests results as in the previous chapter with Test Cloud.

Figure 6-7. *Unit test results in VSTS*

If you combined these types of tests in one build definition, the results would be aggregated here and the combined output would be shown.

Unit Testing Android- and iOS-Specific Code

For unit testing a traditional Xamarin app or some platform-specific code you might have, special templates are available in Visual Studio. If you look back at Figure 6-4, you can also see templates specifically stating Unit Test App for both Android and iOS.

When you add one of these to your solution, you will notice that it differs a bit from regular unit tests. Where regular unit test projects output a library containing your tests, these projects are actual apps. Figure 6-8 shows you my Solution Explorer window in Visual Studio after adding the Android and iOS unit test projects.

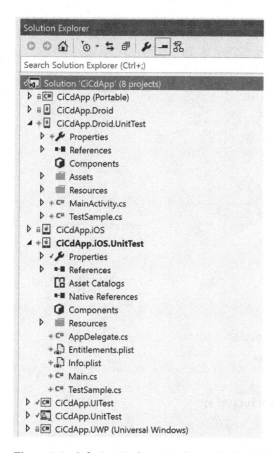

Figure 6-8. *Solution Explorer window with the all the current projects*

When you examine the contents of these projects, you will see that they have everything in there to be fully qualified apps, which can be run on an emulator. Besides that, there is one file in there: the TestSample.cs file.

Running these tests is done through a *test runner* by default. This means that if you run these projects, you are presented with an app that can run the tests for you and provide you with the results. Before you take a look at that, let's take a quick look at the content inside the test classes. Since they are identical in each platform, just one is shown here:

```
[TestFixture]
public class TestsSample
{
    [SetUp]
    public void Setup() { }
```

```
[TearDown]
public void Tear() { }

[Test]
public void Pass()
{
    Console.WriteLine("test1");
    Assert.True(true);
}

[Test]
public void Fail()
{
    Assert.False(true);
}

[Test]
[Ignore("another time")]
public void Ignore()
{
    Assert.True(false);
}

[Test]
public void Inconclusive()
{
    Assert.Inconclusive("Inconclusive");
}
}
```

Once again, you see test fixtures that are similar to what you have seen before. Better yet, the attributes you can work with are the same ones as the tests you wrote for Test Cloud.

■ **Note** The traditional Xamarin unit tests are based on the NUnitLite (Android) and Touch. Unit (iOS) frameworks. There are other testing frameworks out there (for example, xUnit) that can also be used for unit testing Xamarin apps.

To show you how to run the tests, I will just use these sample ones for now. Set either one of these platform unit test projects as the startup project and run it like you would run your app normally. Figure 6-9 shows both the iOS Simulator and the Android emulator side by side with the test runner app.

Figure 6-9. Test runner on Android (left) and iOS (right)

This app searches within the same binary to see whether there are any tests available and lists them within the test runner interface. From there you can select one or more tests and run them from inside the app. Also, the results are presented to you so you can examine the outcome.

While the test runner will suffice for running the tests locally, it imposes a problem when implementing this way in an automated pipeline environment. You cannot run an app, fire the tests through there, and fetch the results from an emulator window.

These tests can be automated, but it takes some effort. Also, for Android it is easier than iOS. For more information on how to set this up, please refer to https://spouliot. wordpress.com/2012/04/02/touch-unit-automation-revisited/ for iOS and https://developer.xamarin.com/guides/android/troubleshooting/questions/ automate-android-nunit-test/ for Android.

Other Test Types

When you scroll through the other build steps available to you in VSTS, you will notice that there are other types of tests available. Although they are useful, they are not suitable to use with mobile applications. The kinds of tests you will find are load testing, performance testing, and functional tests. The latter does, in fact, do the same as Test Cloud, but targeting mostly web applications and even desktop applications.

Like with a lot of mobile apps, you will probably have some form of API back end to feed your app with data. For these kinds of applications, you can still set up a continuous pipeline and have them tested and deployed in an automated way.

■ **Tip**   There are a lot of good resources for more general continuous integration and delivery and the processes around them. One in particular that also focuses on Microsoft technologies is *DevOps on the Microsoft Stack* by Wouter de Kort.

Final Thoughts

In this chapter, you learned how to incorporate UI tests as part of your automated builds. The results are conveniently reported in VSTS where you can inspect them in a unified and clear way.

In addition, you looked at how to write some basic unit tests and make them part of your build definitions. When multiple types of tests are executed in one build definition, the results will be aggregated so you do not have to look in more than one place to gather the results. For Xamarin.Android and Xamarin.iOS projects, platform-specific unit tests projects are available; however, they are not well suited to run in an automated fashion. Because of this, I recommend you use the regular unit test project whenever possible. If the design of your projects is done right, you should be able to implement it even on traditional Xamarin projects.

CHAPTER 7

■ ■ ■

Preparing for Distribution

In the earlier chapters of this book, you learned how to set up automated builds and how to enrich them with tests. Starting in this chapter, you will learn about continuous delivery.

Now that you know how you can build your code automatically and have several quality assurance methods in place, you can step up your game. Continuous delivery is the logical extension of everything you have learned so far. An application is basically nothing until it is in the hands of users, so distributing it to them and getting their responses is extremely important.

I remember the first time I launched an app to a store. A lot of work went into it, and I was finally happy with how everything looked and functioned, so I submitted it. It was a Windows Phone app, and at the time, reviews were not in place yet, and HockeyApp was not born. So, when I got an e-mail that my app was now online and everyone could download it, I was pretty thrilled. How many people were downloading it? Did it work the way I intended? What was going on? But as you might imagine, it stayed quiet. Then (and even now) the download numbers came in delayed by a day or more, and people, certainly strangers, are not always inclined to provide you with (constructive) feedback.

To get any feedback at all, I messaged some friends and family members to get some kind of response. Within a few minutes I got word that the app crashed right at startup. My mind was going into overdrive; how can that be? I tested it, even on a physical device. I had no clue at the time. That is when I learned that a tool like HockeyApp is indispensable. Not only can you get feedback right away, but when things go wrong, you also can find out *what* is going wrong and where to look for it.

If, like me, you have distributed or deployed software before, you probably know it can be a repetitive, meticulous, and sometimes tedious job. This is not what humans are great at. But since distributing and deploying involves computers and systems tied together, they are perfect candidates for automation.

In this chapter, you will take a look at HockeyApp, the distributing service now owned by Microsoft. I will give you a quick overview of everything it offers you, and then I will cover all the prerequisites you need to send your app from VSTS to HockeyApp. Since I am focusing on Microsoft technologies, HockeyApp will be the focus, but of course there are other options such as Bitrise and Fastlane. The appendix of this book describes a few alternatives to HockeyApp.

© Gerald Versluis 2017
G. Versluis, *Xamarin Continuous Integration and Delivery*,
DOI 10.1007/978-1-4842-2716-9_7

A First Look at HockeyApp

The services of HockeyApp have been around for about a decade now. The core functionality is the distribution of apps, but HockeyApp has also ventured into the world of metrics, crash reports, and user feedback.

When Microsoft acquired HockeyApp in 2014 and Xamarin in 2016, HockeyApp and Xamarin Insights had some overlap in functionality. While HockeyApp was focusing on distribution and crash reporting, Insights was more about metrics, following a user's path throughout the app, and crash reporting. You can imagine that these two products combined can be a powerful tool for a business or developer to track an app out in the wild.

At the time of this writing, the transition from Insights to HockeyApp is not complete yet; customers lucky enough to have an Insights account can continue to use it, but Insights is not accepting any new customers. However, you can sign up for HockeyApp right now, just without the great-looking statistics that Insights has to offer.

But the transition does not stop there. At the end of 2016 Microsoft announced Visual Studio Mobile Center. In time, this will be the hub for everything mobile. Here you can distribute your app, as well as see your Test Cloud results and even establish an automated CI/CD pipeline in a very user-friendly way. Mobile Center, however, will not replace VSTS; it will be more like a stepping stone to the fully featured VSTS. You can learn more about Mobile Center in the appendix.

To see what HockeyApp has to offer, you will look at its four main functionalities: distribution, crash reports, feedback, and user metrics. Then you will start preparing for the continuous delivery part of things and start defining your apps in HockeyApp.

Distribution

Getting your app to your end users or testers is important. As you may remember, one of the main things you want to achieve here is to have the shortest feedback cycle possible. This way you will know when something is wrong early on so it is easier to fix.

Going through the hoops of distributing can be a troublesome process. You have to go to each vendor's separate app store, upload your binary, and maybe wait for the company to review it; at every step there are multiple things that can go wrong. This can be a serious delay in your development cycle.

Also, each app store has its own set of features. For example, while Google has multiple ways to recruit testers and put them in separate target groups, Apple has only internal and external testers who must be invited manually. Google has A/B testing, but Apple and Microsoft do not have anything like that.

To provide a unified way for you to distribute your apps, HockeyApp was born. HockeyApp allows you to upload new versions of your app and distribute them instantaneously. Because distribution happens outside of the regular app stores, you can push your app to your end users or testers right away.

Also, HockeyApp has extensive user and group management. You can divide people into groups, work with tags, and assign people different roles such as developer, member, or tester, each with their own permissions.

- Developers can add apps, change all the details, and upload new versions; basically, they are the admins.

- Members can view all the data of the app but not edit it. They can, however, answer to feedback that comes in from users.

- Testers can download and install the app and test it.

If you have developed for iOS before and worked with test versions, you might know that you need to collect the device ID for each device that you want to include in your testing. This ID is known as the unique device identification (UDID). When you collect a new UDID, a new build must be created and rolled out. While the last part is not going away, you still need to create a new build whenever you add a new UDID, but HockeyApp does help you with collecting the device ID. Whenever a user creates an account on their device, with Safari, the UDID will be collected automatically. This is a great gain since finding the ID can be a hard process for the user.

■ **Note**   For an easy alternative way to collect a UDID, please refer to Chapter 9.

Recruiting testers is something HockeyApp can facilitate for you as well. There are basically two ways of approaching your audience: by invitation or by letting them sign up themselves. If you invite the users, you automatically have full control over which specific person you invite and when. In the other case, you set up a public site to which users can navigate and sign themselves up. You still have some control over the maximum number of testers and whether you have to approve their application first. With this method you can set up a full public test if that is what you are after.

All in all, HockeyApp has a lot of great features that can help you get your app out there. You will see its features in a bit more in detail later in this chapter when you set up your apps.

Crash Reports

Another thing that HockeyApp can be used for is crash reporting. Implementing is simple; just install the HockeyApp SDK, maybe add one line of initialization, and that is it!

Whenever an unhandled exception happens, HockeyApp will catch it and turn it into a crash report for you. Not only does it inform you that a crash happened, it will also supply you with the full symbolicated stack trace. But it does not stop there; if the data is available, it will also tell you to which user it happened and what the device specifics are. This way, you have all the information available to fix the bug even before a user has reported it to you.

Automatically, you get statistics about crashes. You can see how many of your users are impacted, when the first and/or last occurrence was, and more. With this information, you can prioritize your bugs and see whether a certain bug was fixed.

The great thing about all these products now being owned by Microsoft is that the integration is profound. For instance, you can set up a link with a bug tracker system so that whenever a crash occurs, it will result in a bug report in the bug administration that you already have in place. The integrations are not limited solely to Microsoft products, however. You can also create a link to Jira, GitHub, Mantis, Trello, and many more products.

Feedback

When your app is on the devices of the users or testers, you probably want to know what they think. The most obvious way to collect feedback from your users is by just letting them send you an e-mail. This will work fine with just a handful of users, but in a company environment or when you have larger numbers of users, administering feedback through e-mail is not the most efficient way.

HockeyApp can help you with that. You can collect feedback through various ways: through the download portal, from right within your app, and via e-mail. The power of collecting your feedback through HockeyApp lies within the aggregation of it. All feedback is available to you through the web interface in an ordered manner. You have the ability to respond to it, at which point the feedback is transformed to a discussion and you can interact with the user about it.

This functionality is useful not only in test versions of your app but maybe even more so in the version that is out in the app stores. Usually your testers are people you know, and they will cut you some slack. When your app is generally available, people will not hesitate to give you a single-star review whenever they do not like something. From there, it is hard to come back.

Just like the crash reports, feedback can have a direct relationship with items in your ticket-tracking or bug-tracking system. You can set up integration with VSTS with just one check box, but a variety other environments are available as well.

The end users are the most important part, and they always know best, so make sure they can reach you in the easiest way possible.

User Metrics

With all the data being gathered by HockeyApp, there are a lot of metrics that can be deduced from it. You can see how many people downloaded your app, how many crashes there were, the number of active users per day or month, and so on.

One functionality that has been ported from Xamarin Insights to HockeyApp is the ability to track specific events. Basically, you add a line of code to identity a certain event, and whenever a user triggers that piece of code, it will report to HockeyApp that the event was triggered. This way, you can measure how often a certain feature is used or even introduce some simple A/B testing to your app.

This functionality can end up collecting data that is privacy-sensitive, so make sure you make it clear to your end users what data is being collected and why.

Setting Up Your App for Delivery

Now that you have seen what HockeyApp can do for you, it is time to get your hands dirty. There are two ways to set up your app within HockeyApp; you can either upload a binary you have or create an app definition and supply a binary later. I will cover the latter option here. If you choose to have a binary and work from there, the procedure is identical for the most part, but some details about your app like the name and icon are already filled in for you.

If you have not already done so, sign up for an account at HockeyApp and make sure you are logged in. With a free account, you will be able to add up to ten apps. Do not let Xamarin fool you into thinking you are just building one app; when it comes to distributing your app, it will still be counted as a separate app for each platform. So, if you have one app that is targeting iOS and Android, it counts as two apps. After those ten apps, you will have to upgrade your account. Participating in testing does not count toward this limit; testing can be done for an unlimited number of apps.

When you are logged in and at your HockeyApp dashboard, you can start adding the first definition. I will explain how to add the iOS app first. Figure 7-1 shows you the HockeyApp dashboard.

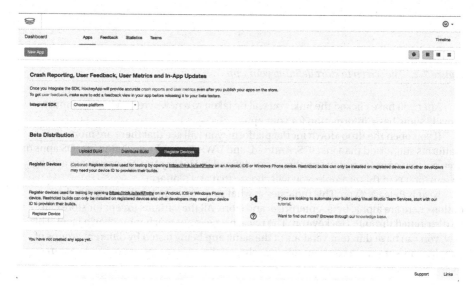

Figure 7-1. *HockeyApp dashboard when no apps are defined yet*

iOS

To start defining the iOS app, or all the apps for that matter, click the New App button in the upper-left corner of the screen. In the pop-up screen that appears, you can either upload an .ipa file or define the app manually by clicking the link in the last bullet. Figure 7-2 shows this screen.

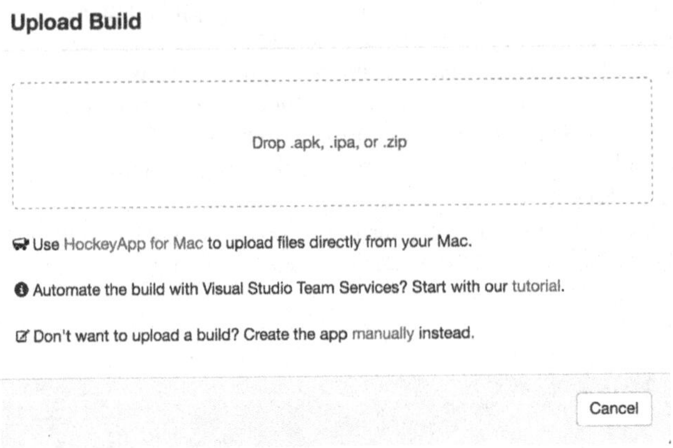

Upload Build

Drop .apk, .ipa, or .zip

⏎ Use HockeyApp for Mac to upload files directly from your Mac.

ⓘ Automate the build with Visual Studio Team Services? Start with our tutorial.

☑ Don't want to upload a build? Create the app manually instead.

Cancel

Figure 7-2. The screen to start defining your app

After you have clicked the link, you will be taken to a new screen where you must provide some basic information for your app.

If you open the drop-down for the platform, you will see that there are more platforms supported than just iOS, Android, and UWP. You can also define macOS apps or even custom ones for a platform that is not defined in HockeyApp. Since you are adding an app for iOS in this example, you will choose that as a platform.

Next is Release Type. This indicates at what stage this app resides; as such, the options here are alpha, beta, enterprise, and store. All the variants except for store can be distributed through HockeyApp. The release type is not much more than a label. This way, you can have different versions of the same app being tested by different groups of people. Another way to go about this is to change the release type as your app matures; this is up to you.

■ **Note**   If you want to have multiple release types simultaneously, each one will count as a separate app within HockeyApp.

Mostly this is just a label shown to the end user, indicating what to expect from your app, so do not worry too much about it.

The last thing you need to do is specify a title for your app; this can be different from the name of your app, but I recommend keeping this the same to avoid confusion. Also, you need to supply the bundle identifier. This is the unique identifier for iOS apps, which usually is a backward domain like com.geraldversluis.myawesomeapp. To link the binaries correctly to the definition in HockeyApp, make sure the identifier correspond between your Visual Studio configuration and the value you enter herein HockeyApp. After you have filled in everything correctly, save the changes to make your new app definition final.

After some processing, you will be brought to your app's dashboard page, as shown in Figure 7-3.

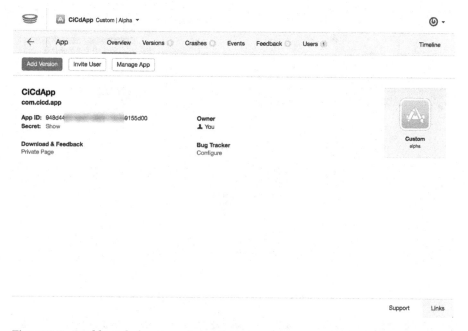

Figure 7-3. Dashboard of your newly created app

On the first page, you see some basic data about your app. When you start distributing or incorporating the HockeyApp SDK into your app, you will also start seeing some statistics about your app on this page.

Furthermore, this is the starting point to all kinds of other information and actions for your app. There are a few references to *versions*. Your app can consist of multiple versions, each having its own set of statistics. This way you have traceability whenever a crash occurs. You can always link it back to a specific version, which correlates with a specific commit of code. Also, the feedback and crashes that are collected are tied to a specific version.

For iOS apps, you must collect the UDID of each device that you want to include in your test, as I mentioned earlier. Whenever you do, you must create a new build and upload it to HockeyApp. Only then the newly added devices are able to download and install the version.

From HockeyApp you can see which device IDs are included in a specific version, and these can be traced back to the users who have signed up.

If you look back to the page shown in Figure 7-3, you will see a field marked App ID. Make sure you note the app ID somewhere because you will need it in the next chapter. Each app will have a separate app ID; this is the way VSTS knows to which app the build should be added.

For now, this is all the configuration you need for your iOS app definition. Let's take a look at how you can integrate the HockeyApp SDK into your code.

Adding the SDK to your app is as simple as just adding the right NuGet package to the project. To add it, go to Visual Studio, right-click the iOS project, and choose Manage NuGet Packages. In the screen that comes up, search for *HockeySDK.Xamarin*. The result should resemble Figure 7-4.

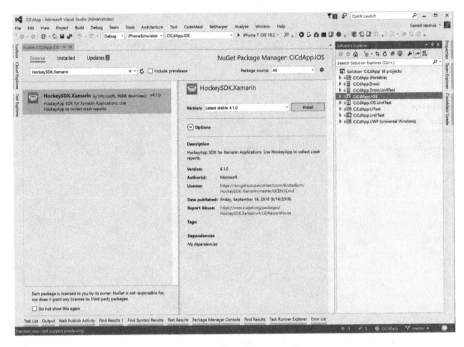

***Figure 7-4.** Installing the HockeyApp SDK to the iOS project*

Install it to the project and wait for the process to complete.

To initialize the SDK, you must tell it to which app ID it corresponds. To do this for iOS, go into the AppDelegate.cs file and add these lines to the FinishedLaunching method:

```
var manager = BITHockeyManager.SharedHockeyManager;
manager.Configure("Your_App_Id");
manager.StartManager();
```

Of course, do not forget to set the right app ID in your own code. This will give you the collection of crashes and metrics automatically. If you do not want to collect metrics or make it dependent on some kind of setting you make available to the user, you can disable it by adding the line manager.DisableMetricsManager = true; before the StartManager method call.

Android

Adding the Android app is mostly repeating the same exercise as you did for iOS. Go back to your dashboard by clicking the HockeyApp icon in the top left and click the New App button again. The screen shown in Figure 7-1 should come up like before.

Just like with the iOS app, you will set the app up manually. The screen shown in Figure 7-5 will appear and is identical as the screen you saw before. This time, as the platform choice is Android, you will see that you now must enter a package name instead of the bundle identifier for iOS.

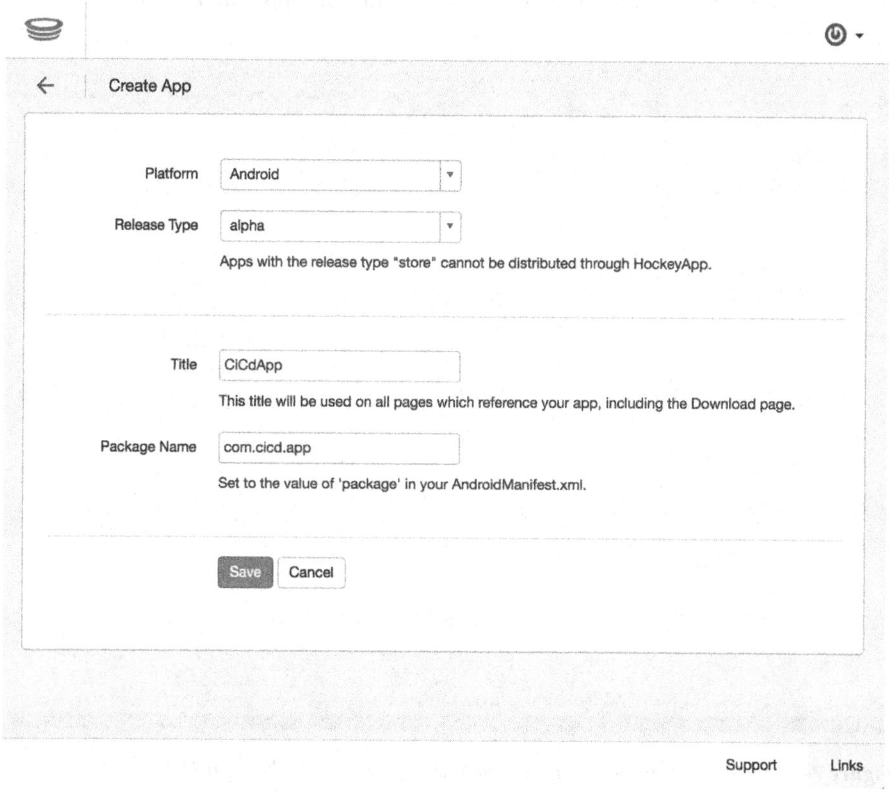

Figure 7-5. *Entering the details of your app*

The package name is like the bundle identifier; it is also formatted as a reverse domain. In my case, it is identical to the one in iOS.

As you know now, the value in the Release field is just a classification. Since the development of the apps for each platform will go hand in hand because we are leveraging Xamarin.Forms, they will both start off at the alpha stage.

When the Save button is clicked, you will be redirected to the dashboard page for this app.

Also, take note of the app ID, as you will need it later.

To incorporate HockeyApp into your code, go to Visual Studio and find the same package as you did for iOS. Then go to the NuGet management of your project and install the HockeySDK.Xamarin package. (The NuGet package management screen was shown in Figure 7-4.)

To initialize the package on Android, you need only one line of code. In your MainActivity.cs file, add the following line in the OnCreate method: CrashManager. Register(this, "Your-App-Id");.

For the SDK to work correctly, you also need to set some permissions. The permissions needed for the HockeyApp SDK are ACCESS_NETWORK_STATE, INTERNET, and WRITE_EXTERNAL_STORAGE. You can set these by going to the project properties in Visual Studio, selecting the Android Manifest tab, and selecting the appropriate boxes. See Figure 7-6.

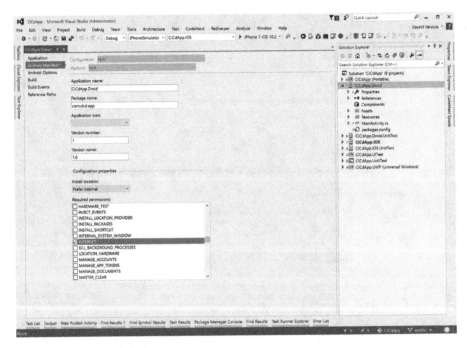

Figure 7-6. *Setting permissions on the Android app for the HockeyApp SDK*

Universal Windows Platform

For Universal Windows, you repeat the same steps as you did for iOS and Android. This time the platform will be Windows, though. The bundle identifier is less strict than for iOS and Android. Since UWP apps do not have an identifier like that, just fill in some unique identifier of your choosing. To keep it similar to your app, it is best to enter the namespace of your app.

Save the new definition and observe the app ID in this app's dashboard page.

Also, integrating the HockeyApp SDK is similar to the apps on Android and iOS. However, for UWP you do not install the HockeySDK.Xamarin package but instead the HockeySDK.UWP package.

To initialize the SDK in your UWP app, you need to add a single line of code to the constructor of your App class, which can be found in the App.xaml.cs file. Add this line of code there, and you should be good to go: Microsoft.HockeyApp.HockeyClient. Current.Configure("Your-App-ID");.

Lastly, you need to set the right permission for your app. Double-click the Package. appxmanifest file and on the Capabilities tab make sure you select the Internet (Client) check box. See Figure 7-7.

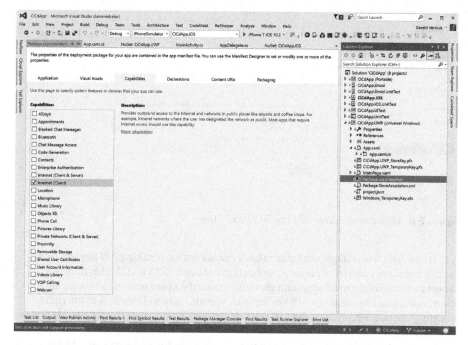

Figure 7-7. *Setting UWP app permissions for the HockeyApp SDK*

Remember that in the free tier of HockeyApp you can have only two apps. If you have already configured the iOS and Android apps, you may have difficulty adding this one as well. Either upgrade your account or make a choice about the platforms you want to use HockeyApp for at this time.

Setting Up VSTS for Delivery

Now that everything is set up on HockeyApp's end, there is some configuration to be done in VSTS. The integration with HockeyApp is not yet available in VSTS by default. Luckily, the VSTS marketplace can help you out.

Before you head over to VSTS, go to your account settings in HockeyApp by pointing to your avatar in the top-right corner and selecting Account Settings from the drop-down. In the resulting screen, find API Tokens in the left-side menu. Here you can create multiple API keys for various purposes. Figure 7-8 shows the screen to do this.

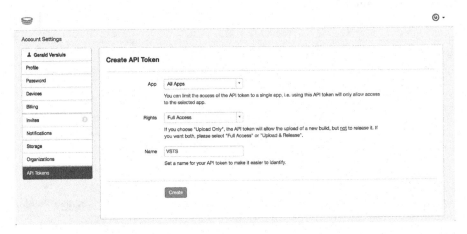

Figure 7-8. Generating a new API key for HockeyApp

There are a few settings available to limit the access the resulting API key will have. For this purpose, which is to create a connection between VSTS and HockeyApp, it is easiest to allow access to all apps and give full access. If you are worried about giving too many rights, you can create an API key for each app and take a closer look at the rights that are given out. Finally, give the API key a descriptive name, most likely a description of where it is used.

Click the Create button. You can see the resulting API key in the overview below this form. Hold on to it for a little bit; you will need it later.

To add the HockeyApp connection, log into your VSTS account and go to the marketplace by clicking the shopping bag icon in the upper-right corner. Search for the HockeyApp extension like I did in Figure 7-9.

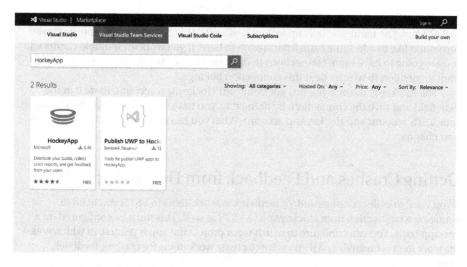

Figure 7-9. *Finding the HockeyApp extension in the marketplace*

Click it to go to the details screen and install it whenever you are ready. This is done by clicking the Install button and selecting the appropriate account on which you would like to install it. If you are not logged into VSTS at the time, you are asked to do so.

After it is installed, go back to VSTS and go to your team project's settings. You can reach the settings by clicking the cogwheel icon or by selecting Services from the drop-down menu to land in the right place immediately. On the left side of the screen, click the New Service Endpoint button and choose HockeyApp, as shown in Figure 7-10.

Figure 7-10. *Creating a link with your HockeyApp account from VSTS*

After clicking the HockeyApp option, a pop-up will be shown asking you for a name and API key. The name is totally up to you; it will probably be just HockeyApp, or maybe you would like to add some extra information in here. If you work for multiple clients and you are going to have more connections to different HockeyApp accounts, you probably want to mention to which client this connection belongs.

The API key is the one you just got from your HockeyApp account. Paste it in the right field and save the connection. By doing this, you have created a connection between your VSTS account and HockeyApp account. What you can do with it you will see in the next chapter.

Getting Crashes and Feedback from HockeyApp in VSTS

If you want to collect crashes and/or feedback as work items in VSTS, you need to configure a connection from HockeyApp to VSTS as well. This must be configured on a per-app basis. You can configure to which team project the app is related, in which area the work item is created, and if you want to create work items for crashes, feedback, or both.

For example, if I wanted to set this up for my UWP app, I would go to my definition for this app in HockeyApp. Click the Configure link under Bug Tracker in the dashboard. This is the option marked in red in Figure 7-11.

Figure 7-11. *Configuring the bug tracker link in HockeyApp dashboard*

In the list of options find VSTS (of course, if you use another system, feel free to use that) and click Configure. You now have to accept the rights you are giving HockeyApp for doing things in VSTS. Inspect the rights that are requested and what they do closely and accept them if you feel comfortable with it. If you do not, this functionality will not be available to you.

After accepting the authorization of HockeyApp with VSTS, you will be taken back to the settings of your app, and you can finish the configuration. If the projects in your account are not showing up, click the Load Projects button and select the team project in which the work items should be created. Figure 7-12 shows the screen for this.

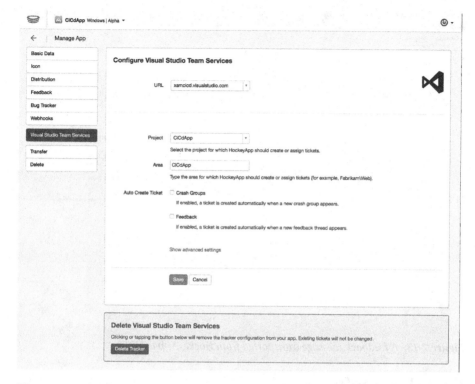

Figure 7-12. Configuring the connection to VSTS for creating work items

Furthermore, you can configure a separate area for the work items to be assigned to. If you are going to use this functionality, I recommend creating an area for each platform. Then configure that platform area here so you can distinguish the crashes and feedback per platform.

Finally, select the boxes for which you want to have work items created. If you select the 'Crash Groups' box, you can also configure a threshold. You can configure it to create a work item when the crash happens a certain number of times or just set it to zero to have the crash added on the first occurrence.

To do a quick test at this point, go to the Feedback tab within your app and create a new discussion. Give it some title and body and send it. Now when you go to VSTS, you should be able to find it as a task. It also works the other way around; if you go to the feedback page in HockeyApp, you will see it has the Tracked status, meaning it has been sent over to VSTS. When you click that tag, you will be taken to the linked work item right away.

In Figure 7-13 you can see how a work item has been created by a feedback message that I composed myself.

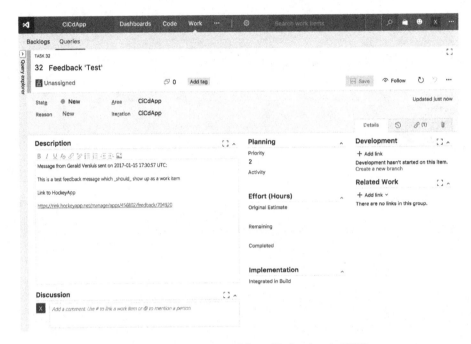

Figure 7-13. A feedback message transported from HockeyApp to VSTS

Final Thoughts

In this chapter, you worked with HockeyApp. You learned that it can be used for a variety of things besides just distributing your app. It is also good at collecting crash reports, gathering user feedback, and providing usage analytics. After that, you started preparations on your apps. You saw that the bundle identifier or package name is a vital part of creating the definitions within HockeyApp. Make sure these are identical on both HockeyApp and your project platforms.

Lastly, you learned how to prepare your VSTS account to use HockeyApp. You installed the HockeyApp tasks for releasing your app, and you linked your accounts together to enable even more integrations such as receiving feedback right in your VSTS account.

In the next chapter, you will start looking at releasing your apps through the configuration you have done here.

CHAPTER 8

■ ■ ■

Releasing Your App

In the previous chapter, you made sure that everything is configured correctly. The last thing you need to do is release actual versions of your binaries. That is what you will learn how to do in this chapter.

You will start by looking at *release definitions*. A release definition is similar to the build definitions you saw in Chapter 3. You can even use the same build tasks in your release definitions. There is, however, one welcome addition: environments. These environments make it possible to deploy or deliver the same release to different (development) environments. You will see how that works in detail later in this chapter.

As part of releasing your app to a specific environment, you will also learn how to distribute to specific groups or even users. Furthermore, I will show you how you can complete the pipeline by deploying to the actual app stores. You will see how to add tasks to VSTS and configure them in such a way that you can send your app right from VSTS to an app store and distribute them to your ultimate targets: the consumers.

Creating a Release Definition

Let's dive right back into VSTS for this. Up until now you have been looking at the Build section of VSTS. But as I have pointed out before, there is a separate Releases section. When you first go there, no releases have been defined yet, as shown in Figure 8-1.

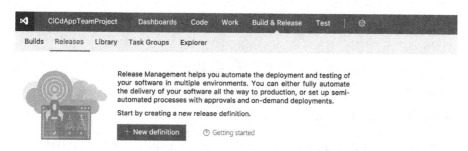

Figure 8-1. Releases section in VSTS

© Gerald Versluis 2017
G. Versluis, *Xamarin Continuous Integration and Delivery*,
DOI 10.1007/978-1-4842-2716-9_8

You'll see a good summary of what you can do with release management in VSTS.

Let's just follow the suggestion and click the "New definition" button. Like when creating a build definition, you can choose between several templates that help you get started. As you go through the list, you will notice how it has templates only for Azure-related releases. Of course, Azure is a likely candidate to release to, and since it is another Microsoft product, rolling out to the Azure platform is a breeze.

However, it is not what you are after; you want to go to HockeyApp and eventually even the app stores. So, pick the empty definition at the bottom of the list and proceed. Figure 8-2 shows the screen that follows. Note that you need to choose a source, and that source is in the form of a build definition. If you open the list, you will see all the build definitions that you have created in the selected team project. This means you cannot have a release definition without having a build definition.

Figure 8-2. *Configuring a release definition*

It is actually not that strange when you think about. Continuous delivery has value only if it is powered by an automated build. If you were to upload binaries yourself, you would still get some benefits, but it would defeat the purpose of continuous delivery. By connecting a build definition to this release definition, the release will automatically know where any artifacts that you provide are available.

In addition to linking the build definition, there are some other minor things that you can configure right away. Specifically, there is a check box to make this release continuous. By selecting it, whenever the linked build definition is triggered and completes successfully, the release definition will be triggered right after that.

Lastly, you again can see the agent queue that is to be used. This time it's not for building but for releasing. As I mentioned earlier, in the release definition you can use the same tasks as in the build definition. That means the agent should have the capabilities to run those tasks as well. If you are only going to push files to a third party, no special capabilities are required. In that case, you can safely use the Hosted agent queue. As you might recall, the hosted agents are the Azure virtual machines that are preconfigured for you. If you use them, you will be charged via the monthly build minutes you have available in your account.

For now, I will keep the configuration as it is and just click the Create button to generate the new build definition.

When that is done, you will be taken to the empty release definition. If you did choose a template earlier, some steps will already be there. Figure 8-3 shows you the newly created release definition. You can think of release definitions like build definitions with different environments at a level above the build steps. So, each environment can have its own steps.

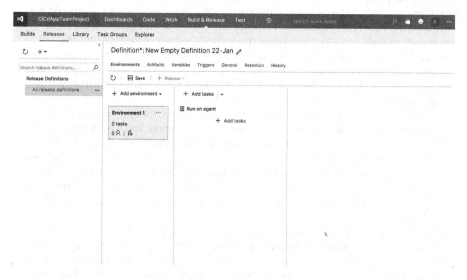

Figure 8-3. *Empty release definition*

On the left side of the screen you will see a list of all the release definitions that are defined for this team project. Since there are none right now, nothing is shown here. On the right side is where the magic happens. The right side of the screen is divided into three columns. From left to right there are the environments, the build steps, and the selected build step configuration.

The build steps column also has the ability to divide steps that are to be executed on the release agent or on the server that you are releasing to. You can create different phases for that, and you can also create multiple phases so you could run something on the agent, then on the server, and then on the agent again. However, at the time of this writing, the server phase has only one build task available: Manual Intervention. The only thing it does is pause the process and notify users to act. Since it is not applicable to releasing apps, I will be describing steps only on the agent.

Environments are traditionally the test, acceptance, and production environments. In most basic form, for instance, you would have a web application, and you take the artifacts from a build and release it to a server by a file copy. That would be one environment. If that succeeds and you are ready for the next step, you would roll on through to the acceptance environment. You would take those same artifacts, copy them to another server or at least another instance, and that is that. The same would go for production. That is exactly what you can do with the environments in release definitions. In one environment add all the steps that are needed to deploy the app to a server, and in the next environment repeat the process or maybe add or skip a few steps.

This is a powerful tool. Not only can you automate the whole process, you can also build a chain of command. You can define users or groups from within your VSTS account, which must give their approval before (or after) releasing a build. Once it is approved, the process will be repeated and deployed to the next environment. Because everything is automated, you can also build in some sanity checks already so you do not have to bother with them yourselves. For instance, when a deploy has been executed successfully to the staging slot, you could run a simple test script to log in and see whether the basic functionality of your application still works. Only then will staging be swapped to production. Or what about executing load tests? When your web application has been deployed, run a load test on it to see whether it still has the performance that you are targeting. The possibilities are endless.

However, for apps it is all less comprehensive. An app is not a public application that runs on a server and that you can just execute scripts upon. You would need to have the actual binaries, like with Test Cloud. So, deploying for apps comes down to different stages of audiences that you distribute them to. Therefore, the environments will be just HockeyApp (or could be HockeyApp multiple times targeting different users), and the final environment will be an app store. You will learn how you can target different groups of people in the next section. For now you'll look at how you can configure a first deploy to HockeyApp.

As a starting point, add a task to the current environment by clicking the Add Task button in the center column, as depicted in Figure 8-3. On the Deploy tab, find the task named HockeyApp; this is part of the extension you installed in Chapter 7. Add it to the release definition and close the pop-up window. Figure 8-4 shows the result of this action.

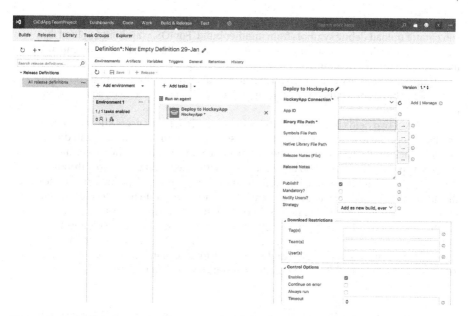

Figure 8-4. *Adding the HockeyApp task to the build definition*

Again, this looks and works exactly the same as for build definitions. Notice the red text and box, indicating that you have not filled in mandatory data for this task. Let's work through that data from top to bottom.

The first field is HockeyApp Connection. This is where you select the connection you made in the previous chapter. From the drop-down box, select the right connection, and that is it. If you have not made the connection yet, you can do so from here by clicking the Add or Manage button.

Next is App ID. Remember that you had to note your app ID while you were looking at the HockeyApp dashboard of your app? This is the place to fill it in. The app ID is platform specific, so make sure you have the right one for the right build here. If you insert the iOS app ID linked to the Android build definition, you will probably get some weird errors. If you are not sure, go back to the HockeyApp dashboard for your app and find the app ID again.

The Binary File Path field is where you select the executable binary file. For iOS, this is the `.ipa` file, for Android it's the `.apk` file, and for UWP it's the `.appxbundle` file. You can use a minimatch pattern here. So, `**/*.apk` is allowed. If you want to enter a full path here, note that it must be relative to the artifact folder. If you are not sure what it should be, click the browse button next to it.

This is the bare minimum of information that is needed to create your first release. Before you create a release, let's go over the rest of the fields as well, so you know what they are there for.

Symbols File Path is the field where you can specify the path to the debug symbols. Although it is not required, I recommend adding it. By adding the debug symbols, your crash reports will be a lot more understandable. If you did not upload them for some reason, you can still add them through the HockeyApp portal if you want. But keep in mind that the debug symbols are linked to this specific set of source code files and binaries. So, you cannot upload debug symbols from another build. For iOS, you should upload the .dSYM file, for Android the mappings.txt file, and UWP uses the .pdb files. You can also include them through a minimatch pattern.

With Native Library File Path, you can also publish native libraries that you might have used. This is some advanced stuff, and I have not needed it to date, so I will skip over this one for now.

The next two fields have to do with *release notes*. To let your users know what has changed since the last time, you can use release notes to inform them. You can do this either by including a text file and entering the path in the first box or by providing text that you supply in the second box. Ideally, in the latter case, you would do it through a variable or get them from somewhere, instead of doing it manually, which kind of defeats the purpose of automating all this. The easiest way to do this is to include a file in your project, which you edit with the newest information. When using a file, a minimatch pattern is allowed. When using a file, separate the release notes for each platform. Although you are working on a Xamarin app and most of the code should be shared, you will reach a point where you have fixed something for one platform and not the other. This way, you can ensure that each platform has its own useful release notes.

■ **Note**   When both the file path to the release notes and the text box with the release notes are filled, the file with the release notes will take precedence over the entered text.

Below the release notes you'll see a few check boxes.

- *Publish*: This allows this version to be downloaded right away. You could also upload a new version and not allow people to download it by not publishing it. This comes in handy, for instance, when you want to release it at a certain point in time later.

- *Mandatory*: You can mark this version as mandatory. The user cannot use an older version anymore; users are forced to update to this version in order to continue using it.

- *Notify Users*: With this you can determine whether you want to notify your users by e-mail that a new version is available. If it is only a minor upgrade, you might want to choose not to spam your users and let them find out for themselves. If it is an important update, you might want to notify them.

Lastly there is the Strategy box. Whenever you upload a version with the same build number, this setting decides what to do. Do you want to replace the version available on HockeyApp, or do you want to ignore the duplicate build number and just deploy it to HockeyApp as a new release? Both options have some pros and cons. When reporting test results, it can be useful to know the build number, so when you have duplicates, you still do not know which exact version the user is talking about. The same goes for replacing the build: how do you know the user has the new or old version with this build number? If you ask me, I say you should try to avoid duplicate build numbers altogether.

The other fields will be described in the next section about deploying to specific users or groups.

You can give the environment a useful name by clicking the environment label. For now, I will stick with HockeyApp. One thing that is different from build definitions is how you name your definition. Build definitions allow you to (re)name it when you save it; for release definitions a name is already suggested. Change it to something meaningful by clicking the pencil behind the current name above the release tasks. Now save the definition and you are ready to release! In Figure 8-5 you see the filled-in HockeyApp task with all the information I have described. In my case, I have configured the Android release.

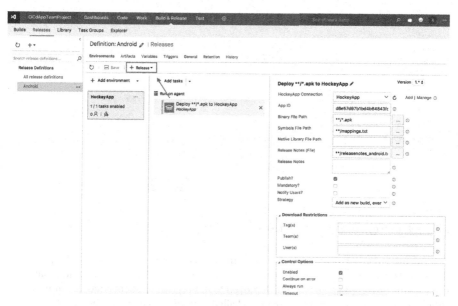

Figure 8-5. *Your first release definition, ready to go*

To create a release and see whether everything is configured correctly, click the Release button marked by the arrow in Figure 8-5. You have the option here to either create a release right now or create a draft release. You want to release right now, so choose the first option. In the pop-up screen that comes up, you need to configure some things. This is needed because you are triggering this release manually. If it was triggered automatically, VSTS would know everything that is needed in this form and would create a release for you. You will learn how to do this later on in this chapter.

Figure 8-6 shows the pop-up that appears. The only thing you really need to configure here is which artifacts are linked to this release. As you learned earlier, a release definition is always linked to a build definition. Because of this link, you can easily select a build number representing these artifacts from the drop-down. Again, when this release is triggered automatically by a build definition, it is apparent that the artifacts from that build are the ones to use for a release, so this will not be necessary. Choose a build from the drop-down (preferably the last one) and click the Create button. After you do, a small bar will be shown that lets you know the release has been created. You can click its name to navigate right to it or find it on the release's overview screen.

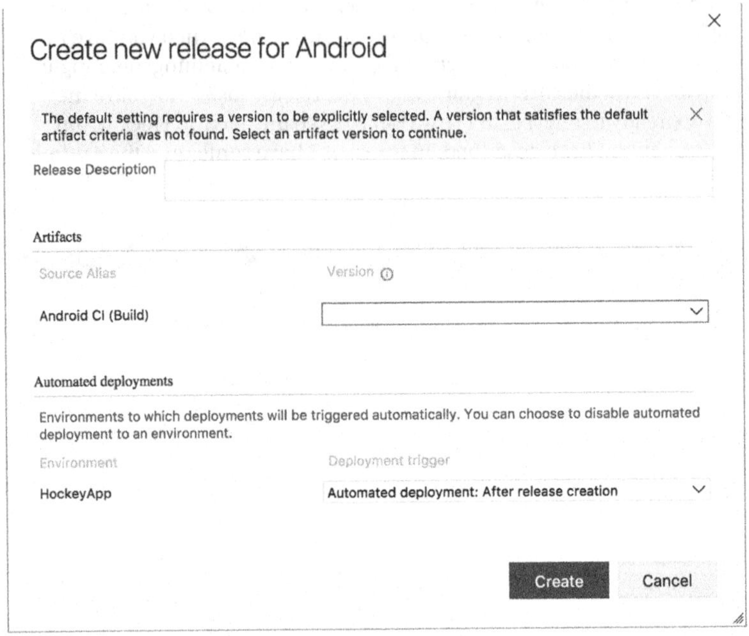

Figure 8-6. *Triggering a manual release*

On the screen of the current deployment for this release, you can follow the progress. You will see a list of environments (only one in your case right now), and behind that is a small status box. It will go from Not Deployed to In Progress to Succeeded. If something should go wrong, the status will change to Failed, and the screen will show what went wrong below the environments.

In addition, there is some more information such as which work items are related, when a release was triggered and completed, and so on. You can see a deployment in progress in Figure 8-7.

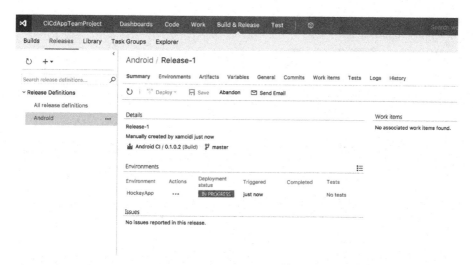

Figure 8-7. *Deployment to HockeyApp in progress*

■ **Tip** Your deployment might fail if the release notes file and/or debug symbols files are not found. Even while they are not mandatory to supply, when you do fill in these files, the files must exist.

After the deploy succeeds, you can go to HockeyApp, and in the app dashboard you should now see the version that you have just deployed. Congratulations, you have just created your first automated release!

You will look at the HockeyApp side of this release later in this chapter; for now let's go back to the release definition and look at some more configuration in-depth.

Just like the build definitions, release definitions have several sections. They are actually quite similar. If you look at Figure 8-8, under the definition name and above the configuration part of the screen, you'll see the sections Environments, Artifacts, Variables, and so on.

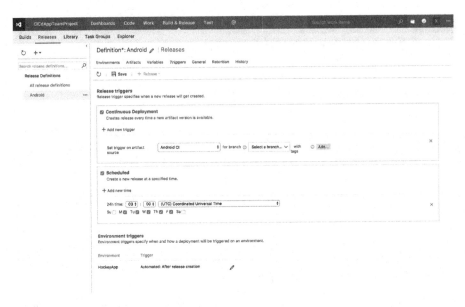

Figure 8-8. *Triggers in a release definition*

I will not discuss all of them in detail, but I will give a brief description of each.

- *Environments*: This is the part that you have already handled. Here you can configure everything that has to do with how the release flows through different environments.

- *Artifacts*: Here you can configure to which build definition this release is linked to. For more advanced scenarios, you can link multiple build outputs to one release and work with them.

- *Variables*: In this section, you can configure variables, just like the ones in build definitions. There is, however, one addition. Here you can make use of *variable groups*. These groups are nothing more than a container for a set of variables. For instance, if you use variables specific to your HockeyApp account, you can create a variable group, configure all the variables there, and link the group to multiple releases. That way, you do not have to duplicate variables and their values. Note that variable groups work only within one team project.

- *Triggers*: Figure 8-8 shows this section. Again, this is similar to the build definition triggers. The scheduled trigger is identical. The Continuous Deployment trigger creates a trigger that links directly to a build definition. Whenever a build definition is triggered (either through a schedule or through a continuous integration trigger), this release will be triggered right after that. You can fine-tune it a bit more by selecting a branch and/or tags that the trigger should respond to.

- *General*: Under the General section there is just one setting: the name that is given to a release. By default the format is `Release-$(rev:r)`, which literally spells out the word *Release-* and postfixes it with an incrementing number, which is the revision. You can change it to whatever you like and use (built-in) variables.

- *Retention*: With the settings under Retention you can influence how long the artifacts for this release are saved.

- *History*: Lastly, on the History tab you can see who made which changes in this release definition when. This is an audit log of every change that is made in this definition.

Most of these sections and settings are self-explanatory or you have already learned about them in previous chapters about build definitions. In the next section, you will look at how to add multiple environments and build an approval structure so users can roll out the release to different environments.

Building a Chain of Command Between Environments

Let's go back to the release definition and into the Environments section. Earlier, when you configured the environment, one environment was already there. Now you are going to add a new environment by clicking the "Add environment" button above the list of environments. When you do, there are two choices: clone the selected environment or create a new one. With the first option, an exact copy is made with a new name, while the second option gives you the option to select another template to start from, which you can then configure from scratch. For the sake of speed, let's clone the one you have already.

In either case, you are presented with a screen where you can configure some options already. These options have to do with predeployment approval and the trigger. Just keep the default settings and finish the process. You should now have two environments with identical configurations, only their names are HockeyApp and Copy of HockeyApp. You can rename them if you want, but you will look at how to name them with more meaningful names in the next section of this chapter when you are going to deploy to specific users and groups.

When you take a look at the squares that represent your environments, you will notice three dots in the upper-right corner, next to the name of the environment. When you click the dots, a context menu appears and presents you with a couple of options. Clicking the first option, "Assign approvers," presents you with a pop-up screen, as shown in Figure 8-9. In the pop-up screen, you can also reach the sections for the other options in the context menu.

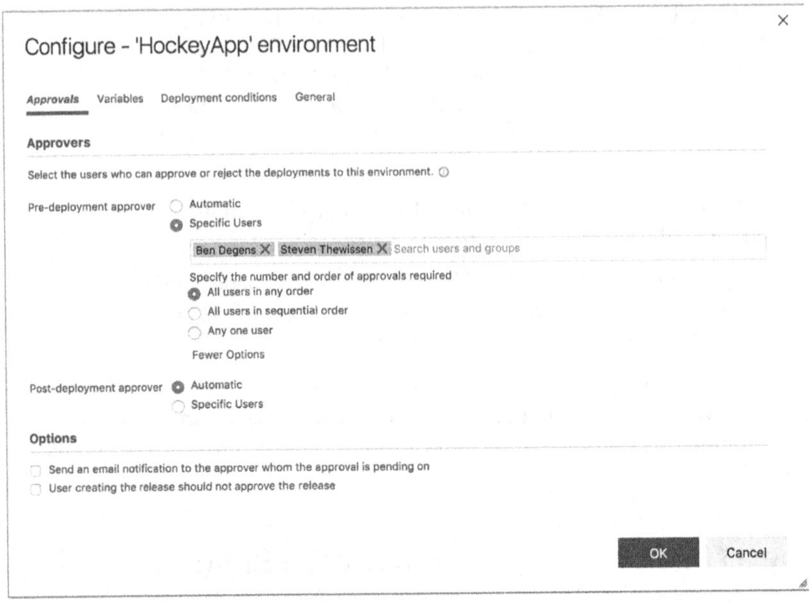

Figure 8-9. Configuring approvals for your environment

The first tab of this screen is where you can configure the approvals. While the configuration is easy, it is very powerful. The default configuration is to approve a deploy to the selected environment automatically. This means that a deploy is automatically executed on this environment, and when it is successfully done, it will also be automatically be approved and repeated on the next environment if there is one.

However, if you want to have some approval or chain of command in place, you can do so. In either the pre- or post-deployment, you can select the radio button for specific users. When you do, you can add one or multiple users (these users must be in your VSTS account *and* the current team project).

After adding the users, you give them some more control over how the approval process should go. You can select whether it is enough that one of the users needs to approve and whoever is fastest wins. The other options specify that *all* users must approve. The nuance in this is that they can do it in any order, or it can be in the specific order that you put the users in the text box.

In my case, all users must approve in any order, but Ben and Steven both have to give their go-ahead on this.

You can create numerous scenarios. Imagine that you work at a company with dedicated testers. With this functionality, you can create a first environment that sends the app to HockeyApp and in that group are the developers. Deploying could be done automatically triggered from an integration build on the main branch. With this a new test version is released, and the developers (or a specific subset) get it first to see whether anything is wrong. But then it halts. In the post-deployment (or pre-deployment of the next environment), one or more developers have to approve. When they do, the deployment is repeated, but this time it will be made available to the testers. They can run their scripts, do everything to make sure that the quality of your app is still guaranteed, and then give their approval as well. Another environment could be to deploy it to an actual app store. This way, the developer does not have to remember to prepare a (separate) release.

At the bottom, there are some more options; one is for notifying the people that the approval is dependent upon by e-mail. The other option says that the user creating the release (or, the user triggering the release by doing a commit, etc.) cannot be an approver as well. With this, you can guarantee that other people have looked at this new release as well. By enabling this option, you prevent that one stubborn developer who thinks he can do it all by himself from pushing out a release by himself.

Since the concept of variables has been handled already, I will skip that for this screen. Also, the General section has options that are easy to understand, so lastly I will show you what configuration is available on the "Deployment conditions" tab. Figure 8-10 shows this screen.

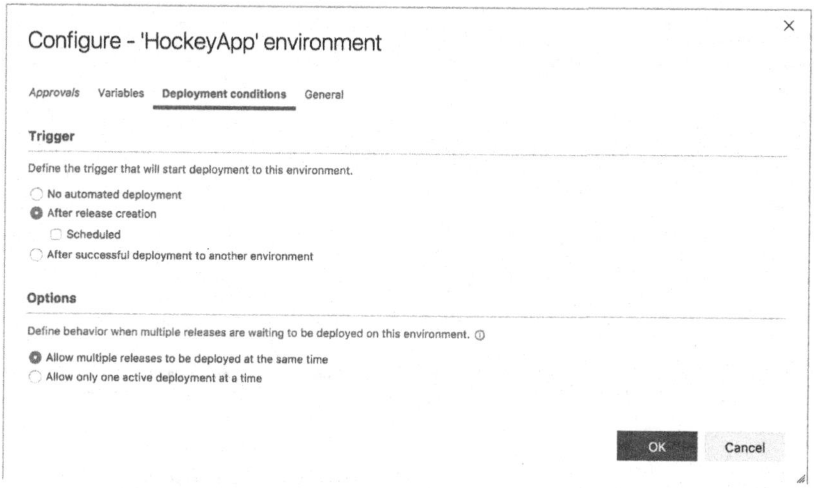

Figure 8-10. *Configuring deployment options*

In this screen, you can configure conditions that must be met before a release will commence. With the trigger condition, you can specify whether a release is triggered automatically. If it is, you can schedule it or let it run after a successful deployment to the previous environment.

Under Options, you can determine the behavior when multiple releases are running at the same time. You can have them deployed simultaneously or consecutively, or you can take only the most recent release and deploy that one.

■ **Note** All these options are tied together. Before you start setting up different environments and releases, create a plan on when and how you want to release versions and who should approve of them. VSTS does a good job of guiding you through the different options and warning you of any implications, but it is still good to know what you are doing.

When a release is triggered, you will see the different environments that are in your release definition. Figure 8-11 shows this status.

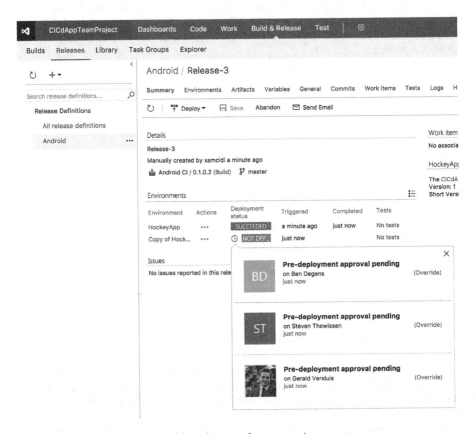

Figure 8-11. *Awaiting approval for release to the next environment*

If one of these users logged in under their account (I am logged in under another account in this screenshot), they would have the ability to approve or deny this release right here. Depending on the configuration, they would also have had an e-mail message notifying them that action is required. Approval can also be done directly from that e-mail and several other places that indicates the status of this release.

When approving a release, you can defer the release to the next environment, and you can specify a date and time in the future. At this date and time the next step in this release will commence.

When all conditions are met, the process is repeated for that environment with the same artifacts as before.

All this time I have been talking about approving the version, but what happens when you reject one? Nothing exciting I'm afraid. You can reject a release and add some comments as to why you came to that decision. If someone has set an alert on this action, they will be notified, but it is recommended that you as the person with the authority to reject actually take the action for a follow-up. Create one or more work items to fix the issues that you were experiencing and wait for another release to come along.

Deployment to Specific Users or Groups

One scenario that fits perfectly into the multiple environments functionality is to bring your app to specific users each time. That is something that can easily be done with HockeyApp.

As I described earlier in this chapter, you might want to identify different groups to which you can add users. For instance, for projects I am working on, I mostly create three groups: developers, testers, and management. When a version is released, first it goes to the developers. This is just a sanity check, making sure the build still works when the code is signed and running on a physical device. When everything seems all right and the approval process has been satisfied, it rolls out to the testers.

They unleash their scripts and regression tests, and if everything is to their satisfaction, they approve this version and let it flow through to management. Of course, if a version is not approved, it will be rejected, rework will commence, and the whole process starts over.

To learn how you do this, let's take a look at the HockeyApp dashboard, as shown in Figure 8-12.

Figure 8-12. *HockeyApp dashboard with your apps*

In the upper bar, you can see a couple of options: Apps, Feedback, Statistics, and Teams. It is the last one that you are interested in. When you click Teams for the first time, you will get some introduction text about how you can use this feature. That is exactly what you are going to find out!

Also on this screen is a button you can click to create a new team, as shown in Figure 8-13. A team is nothing more than a name and the users who belong to it. So, name your teams appropriately; in my case I start with the developers. If you have users to put in this group right now, you can invite them by entering their e-mail addresses in the right box and pressing the Enter key.

Figure 8-13. *Creating a new team in HockeyApp*

From here there are two possibilities: you add a new user or you add an existing user who is already known in your HockeyApp account. For the latter group, nothing much will happen, except that they are added to this group.

New users need to create a HockeyApp account, so they will receive an e-mail message no matter what. You can choose to send the same message to existing users as well, to let them know they are now in the new group. You can also add a personal message, but this is not required.

After each user you can specify the role that user should have. These roles were discussed in Chapter 7. There is, however, one more role available here: Manager. This role can do everything a Developer can but can also manage teams.

The last thing you can configure here are *tags*. A tag is just another way to categorize users. Tags can be created by just typing some text in the input box. Whenever you type a comma or space, your tag is created. When your tag is already in the system, it will be presented to you by a suggestion box. Later you can specify users by their tags. Personally, I haven't used tags a lot. But if you can find a use for them, go right ahead!

■ **Note**   The user creating the group is automatically added as a Manager and cannot leave the group. Consequently, he or she will receive notifications about all releases to each group, which can become a lot. You can change this in your account settings, but you cannot leave the group or change your role.

When the team is created, you will be brought back to the overview page of all teams, where your newly created team should now be visible. If you want to make the rest of the teams now, go right ahead.

After you create all the teams you want, you need to gather the team ID. To get it, navigate to a team and look at the URL. It should look something like this: `https://rink.hockeyapp.net/manage/teams/90168/edit`. As you may have guessed, the number in this URL is the ID for this team. Gather all the IDs of all the teams you want to use for your releases. These IDs are used to uniquely identify them. By entering the ID in VSTS, you create a link to this particular group. This way, VSTS knows to which group the new app version must be made.

While you are here, go to the Apps section for a group. You need to link one or more apps to one group. If you do not do this, the users cannot download it. Make sure you check all the apps that you want to associate to this group of people.

Now, you go back to VSTS and into your release definition. Select the first environment and after that the HockeyApp task. There is a section in the configuration that you did not handle yet, when you were here before. You can see it in Figure 8-14.

Strategy	Add as new build, even if the same bu ⌄ ⓘ

▲ **Download Restrictions**

Tag(s)		ⓘ
Team(s)		ⓘ
User(s)		ⓘ

▲ **Control Options**

Enabled	☑
Continue on error	☐

Figure 8-14. Configuration for tags, users, and teams in HockeyApp

With the knowledge you now have, you know what you can do with these fields. For the teams and users, you need the IDs of those entities. Getting the user ID is roughly the same as getting a team ID; navigate to a user and find the ID in the URL.

You can configure multiple users or groups by separating them with comma, for example, 1234, 5678, 90168.

For tags, it works the same, only you input the tags as they are.

You can enter values in each of the fields, but when you do, please note that only users who meet all the criteria are targeted. For each environment, you can enter the users or groups that you want to target for that version. Combined with setting who can approve these releases within VSTS, this makes for a flexible and powerful system to deliver your versions to your users.

To make things a bit more transparent, you can now rename your environments and have them reflect the user group that the environment targets along with the platform it is released to.

Release to the App Store

The ultimate goal is to release the app to the respective platform's app store. This is something that is not supported by default. Luckily, the VSTS marketplace comes to the rescue!

Just like you did for HockeyApp, find these extensions in the marketplace and add them to your account: Windows Store Automation, Apple App Store, and Google Play. There are some variations available, but they should all work similarly. I will now show you how to configure the task for each store. Since I have been releasing the Android app up until now, I will start with configuring the Google Play Store. However, I will not explain how to set up release definitions in detail because they are all the same except for a few details.

Google Play Store

In the release definition you have used so far, I will add one last environment, which will release the app to the Google Play Store. In this environment, I will add the task that you just installed from the marketplace, and immediately you will see some red fields coming up, indicating you have some work to do, as shown in Figure 8-15.

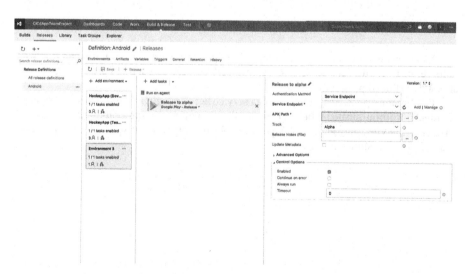

Figure 8-15. *Configuring the release task for Google Play Store*

Just like you had to do for HockeyApp, you need to set up a service endpoint for the Google Play Store. Before you do this, you need to go into your Google Developer Console account and set up an API key.

So, head over to the Developer Console on `https://play.google.com/apps/publish/`. Log into your account and find the Settings tab in the left menu. In the screen that now appears, select API access, and a screen like Figure 8-16 should be visible. There is some information on security that you need to consider, so read it carefully and make sure you are understanding what you are doing.

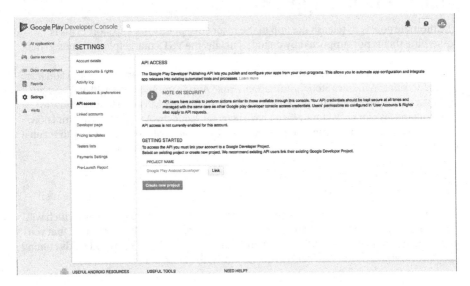

Figure 8-16. *Creating a API key for your Google Play Store account*

You now need to create a project on the Google Developer Console. You can do this automatically by clicking the "Create new project" button. After a bit of processing, there should be a linked project available.

On the same page, near the bottom, a service account will be listed. These accounts are ideal to communicate on behalf of an application or system rather than an end user. First, click the View in Google Developer Console link after the entry, which will take you to a new page, as shown in Figure 8-17.

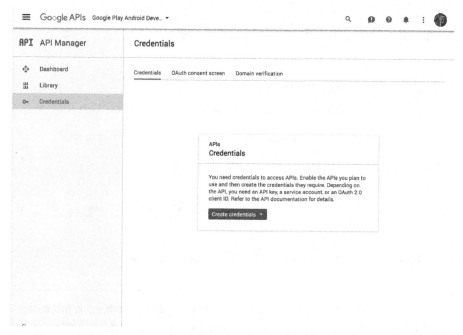

Figure 8-17. *Generating the API key credential*

Click the "Create credentials" button and choose "Service account key" from the drop-down menu that appears. On the next screen, select the service account from the drop-down menu (there should be only one), make sure the Key type is set to JSON, and click the Create button. A JSON file will be downloaded, which contains the private key you can use to connect to the Google Play Developer Console.

Back in the API access settings, click the "Grant access" button and make sure the role is set to Release Manager. Save these settings, and you are good to go.

The last thing you need to do is create the app entry in your Google Play account. Go back to the "All applications" tab and click the "Add new application" button. This process should be self-explanatory, and you probably have created some apps before, so I will not go through this in detail. Most important is that the package identifier (the reversed domain, for example com.yourdomain.app) corresponds with the one you configured in your AndroidManifest.xml file. That is the way the .apk file is linked to the app entry in the Google Play Developer Console. The downside is that you need to upload at least one .apk file with the same package identifier to this app entry; there is no way to preconfigure the package identifier other than to upload an .apk file. To be clear, it is *not* possible to provide the first version this way.

With all the prerequisites covered, let's go back to VSTS and finish the configuration there. Right behind the Service Endpoint field click the Add button. In the pop-up that comes up you can configure the endpoint right away. Enter a descriptive name and open the downloaded JSON file. In the file, find the values behind private_key and client_e-mail. Fill out the e-mail field with the value from client_e-mail and the private key in the other field. Make sure you do not copy the quotes, but *do* copy everything from beginning to end in case of the key. For an example, see Figure 8-18. Save the configuration, and that is that.

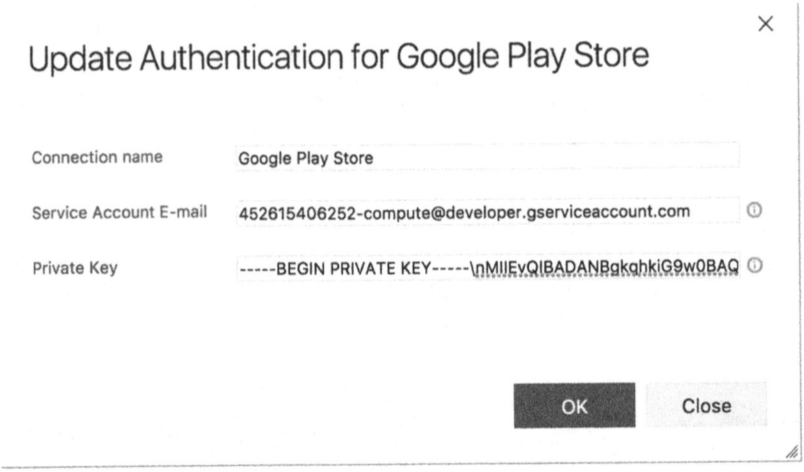

Figure 8-18. *Sample service endpoint configuration for Google Play*

■ **Tip** You can use the downloaded JSON file as an authentication method. In that case, check in the file as part of your repository, and point the configuration of the Google Play task to that file.

The next thing you need to configure is the path to the .apk file. Like with all the other boxes to supply files, you can work with variables and minimatch patterns, so make sure you enter a path that points to your signed and zipaligned .apk file.

The last important thing here is the Track field. In the Google Play Store, you have multiple tracks: alpha, beta, production, and rollout (short for staged rollout). You can have different versions of your app in each track, so you can offer them to a certain set of users of your choosing. Basically, this functionality is the same as that of HockeyApp, so you can also choose to deploy to the Google Play Store immediately and let your users get their versions through there. I think alpha, beta, and production speak for themselves, but rollout needs a bit of explaining. With rollout, you can specify a percentage of your users (from 5 to 50 percent), which are then selected randomly to receive the new version you specify.

In Figure 8-19 you can see that I have added yet another environment. This one contains a task to promote my app in the Google Play account. This way, you do not have to upload the .apk file again, but you can promote the current .apk file from one track to another. The only thing you need is the package identifier in this case.

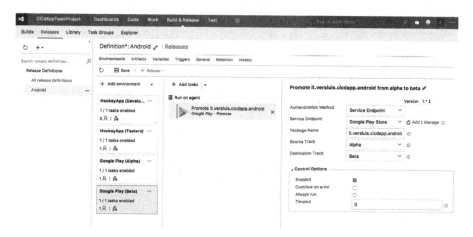

Figure 8-19. *Finalizing the release definition for Android*

If you save this and create a new release, you should be able to get your first version to the Google Play Store!

Of course, this is just one example of how to orchestrate it; there are limitless variations to think of yourself. How you set this up is up to you and the requirements you have.

■ **Tip** The release task for Google also allows you to send the metadata along with the binary of the app. The metadata includes all the screenshots, store descriptions, and so on. This way you can also make this part of your repository and update it right from your IDE. For more information on how to do this, check out the documentation of the extension at `https://marketplace.visualstudio.com/items?itemName=ms-vsclient.google-play`.

Windows Store

For the Windows Store, I will repeat roughly the same process. The easiest way to get this up and running is to clone the previous release definition and just edit the app IDs, group IDs, and so on. The most important part when you clone a definition is to not forget to change the reference to the build definition under Artifacts.

The biggest change will happen, of course, when you get to the step where you are going to deploy to the Windows Store. If you have cloned the release definition, delete the task for that app store and add Publish to Windows Store instead. The result will look something like Figure 8-20.

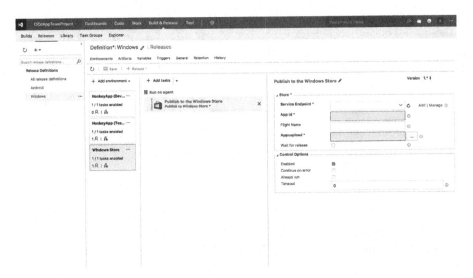

Figure 8-20. *Adding the Windows Store task*

The first thing you need to do is set up the service endpoint for this app store. To do this, you need to have your Windows Store Developer account backed by an Azure Active Directory (Azure AD). This process can be started from the developer account dashboard. Log into it, go to the account settings, and continue to "Manage users." Here you can link your account to any Azure AD you have already set up or create a new one right there. For more details on the how to do this, take a look at the documentation by Microsoft: https://docs.microsoft.com/en-us/windows/uwp/publish/manage-account-users.

When you have this set up, you need to get three things to create the service endpoint: a tenant ID, a client ID, and an API token. After you have associated the Azure AD, go back to the "Manage users" page and click Add Azure AD Applications. Follow the instructions on the screen and add the application that represents the app or service that you will use to access the app submissions, in this case VSTS. Make sure that you assign the Manager role to it.

Again, return to the "Manage users" page, click the name of the application that you have just added, and copy the fields in the Tenant ID and Client ID boxes. Finally, click the "Add new key" button and make note of the key that is presented to you. Take a good look; you will get to see it only once.

With this data, go back to VSTS, create the service endpoint, and make sure it is selected.

Just like for the Google Play Store, you cannot submit your first version of the app through VSTS. You need to have an entry in your developer account already. To do this, go into your account and on the dashboard click the "Create a new app" button. After you have completed the process, when you go into the app, you can see the app ID in the URL. It should look like this: https://developer.microsoft.com/en-us/dashboard/apps/PBF330VJ289. Take this app ID and put that in the right field as well.

The last mandatory field is the Appxupload field, which needs to be the path (or minimatch pattern) to your binaries that need to get uploaded to the account.

Note the Flight Name field. A *flight* is Microsoft's way of creating different tracks to deploy your app to only a specific set of users.

■ **Tip** Just like for the Google Play Store task, you can provide the metadata along with the binaries of your UWP app. You can find more about how to do this and all the documentation for this task on the extension page at `https://marketplace.visualstudio.com/items?itemName=MS-RDX-MRO.windows-store-publish`.

Apple App Store

With two down, you just have one left, the Apple App Store. Contrary to some other Apple-related processes, this one is easy to implement.

Like before, clone another definition or create a new one. I will just clone a previous one, update the necessary HockeyApp IDs, and start replacing the actual app store task. Make sure you link it to the right artifacts when you clone the definition yourself. After adding the environment for it and adding the Apple App Store Release task, your screen should look similar to Figure 8-21.

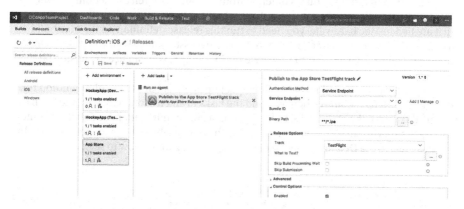

Figure 8-21. *Configuring the Apple App Store Release task*

You can choose to add another service endpoint or connect with your user name and password. However, configuring the endpoint just consists of your user name and password.

After creating and selecting the connection, there are a few routes to take. They depend on whether you want to deploy to TestFlight or production.

If you deploy to TestFlight, your configuration basically is done now. If you want, you can configure a file that contains text that is provided to the user on what to test. Of course, you should make sure that Binary Path contains a valid path or minimatch pattern that points to the .ipa file that is to be distributed. Just like the Google Play task, there is also a task to promote your version, but for the App Store just one promotion is possible: from TestFlight to production.

The other path is to deploy to production right away. To do this, set the Track field to Production. When you do, the Bundle ID field will become mandatory, although it will not appear that way in the UI. Make sure you fill it with the bundle ID that you have specified in your app (which is formatted like the reverse domain).

When switching to the production track, a number of new options appear. While none of them is required, there are some handy functionalities. Like the other stores, you will also have the ability to upload metadata and screenshots along with your binary file. There are also some switches to automatically submit the app for review and release it automatically after it is successfully reviewed. These are all options that should be familiar to you if you have released an app in the App Store before.

To read all about the abilities of this extension, check the documentation page: https://marketplace.visualstudio.com/items?itemName=ms-vsclient.app-store.

Before you can start uploading your version to the App Store, you need to register your app with the store. You can do this through your iTunes Connect account. To do this, log into your account and click the plus button. Fill out the form to create the necessary app record. You should already have created the App Bundle to create the required certificates for building your app in the first place, as described earlier in this book.

If you need any more help on this subject, check out the Apple documentation at https://developer.apple.com/library/content/documentation/LanguagesUtilities/Conceptual/iTunesConnect_Guide/Chapters/CreatingiTunesConnectRecord.html.

There is one last thing that is different from the other two release definitions when releasing to those app stores. Because Apple always uses some very specific techniques that are tied to Mac hardware, you need to run this release definition on the Mac build agent you installed in Chapter 2. Note that this is necessary only when you want to release to the App Store. If you just want to release to HockeyApp, you can use the hosted build agents.

If you have the Mac build agent already set up, it is not hard to let this definition run on it as well. In the column where you add the tasks to an environment, click the "Run on agent" link above the list of tasks. In the right pane, the configuration for the agent comes up. Make sure you set "Deployment queue" to the queue where the Mac agent resides. In my case, that is the Default queue. Reference Figure 8-22 to see how to set it.

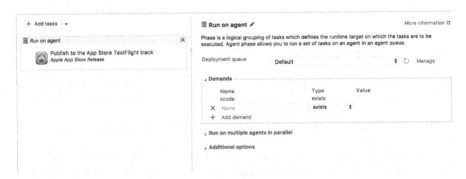

Figure 8-22. *Configuring the release definition to run on the Mac build agent*

■ **Note**   At the time of this writing, two-factor authentication is not supported. If you want to use VSTS to deploy to the App Store, you must disable it.

Final Thoughts

With releasing your apps to the actual stores, your pipeline is complete. You should now have learned everything you need to set up a complete automated building and deployment system. How you want to set things up depends on you. Just be prepared; you will have a lot of trial and error ahead of you before you get it right.

Just try to start small. Go for one platform at first, make it build automatically, then deploy it to HockeyApp, and work from there. Start expanding your builds with tests and more platforms and then deploy to multiple environments and more users. In the beginning, it will feel like you do not gain much time from it, but as you go, you will get the hang of it. And remember, not only time is to gain here, but more important factors are stability and repeatability. Eliminating the human factor (which is more often than not the weakest link in automation systems) is also something you want—no more repetitive tasks and no more making the same mistake repeatedly when releasing an app.

CHAPTER 9

A Closer Look at HockeyApp

In Chapter 7, you made your first acquaintance with HockeyApp. You learned about the features at a glance, and if you followed along with the instructions, you have installed the SDK into your app. Then, in Chapter 8, you saw how to work with different target groups and deploy a version specifically to them.

In this chapter, you will take a closer look at what HockeyApp has to offer you. To start, you will learn how to install your app on a device, distributed through HockeyApp. This will help you understand what end users will see and how they can work with it.

After that, you will see how all the data that is collected can work to your advantage. You will, again, start with the end user and see how feedback can be collected. Subsequently, the rest of the chapter will be about data that is gathered without the user's intervention. This data includes error reports, custom events that you can specify yourself, and user statistics. While there are already a lot of settings in place regarding the privacy of the user, with HockeyApp it is still possible to gather some sensitive information without the user knowing it. Therefore, make sure that you include a clear privacy statement; it is also a good idea to provide some functionality for the user to opt in or opt out of gathering all this data. Depending on where you are releasing the app, this may even be required by law.

To be able to distinguish unique users without collecting details about a user, a unique user ID (UUID) is generated by HockeyApp. This UUID is not affiliated with any of the user's details and is not reused across different apps. There are some details that are stored on the HockeyApp servers in the United States. The data that involves the user includes country and language, but there is also some device data such as device type and OS version. This data is not considered personal identifiable information (PII). If you want more information on the how and why of HockeyApp data collection, please refer to https://support.hockeyapp.net/kb/app-management-2/what-data-is-collected-with-the-hockeysdks-2. Also, the HockeyApp SDK is open source, so you can inspect what is going on yourself.

Installing Your App on a Device

Installing your app through HockeyApp should be an easy-to-understand process. Since end users are its target audience, everything is explained in detail. The thing about users, however, is that they do not always read very well. To be able to support your users while they are acquiring your app, you will take a look at this process.

© Gerald Versluis 2017
G. Versluis, *Xamarin Continuous Integration and Delivery*,
DOI 10.1007/978-1-4842-2716-9_9

There are basically two scenarios possible: you invite the users yourself and they sign up through the e-mail they get, or you set out a public recruitment and users sign up through a link.

In my experience, the first scenario is far more common, especially in a corporate environment where you are part of the development team and you have some testers. Therefore, I will explain only this scenario. The process of providing a public link is mostly identical.

In the previous chapter, you learned how you to add users to groups. When the user is not already in the HockeyApp account, an invitation will automatically be sent. Of course, you are not obligated to use groups. You can use individual users just as well.

To do that, log into HockeyApp and navigate into the app that you want to invite a user for. This means you need to know what kind of phone they are using. Since you are inviting the user, you probably know who it is and what platform they are using. When in the app dashboard, click the Invite User button in the upper bar, as shown in Figure 9-1. In my case I have gone into the iOS app.

Figure 9-1. *Inviting a user to the iOS app*

The screen that appears next is similar to the screen when you add someone to a group, but you invite just one user here. Follow the instructions on the screen; most importantly, enter their e-mail address and select their role. You can also assign tags to this user and enter an optional custom message for them. After you have filled out the form to your liking, save it, and the user will be informed by e-mail.

Note that if you want the same user to be part of multiple apps, you must invite them for each app separately.

Figure 9-2 shows the e-mail that the user will receive. There will be slight variations for the different platforms, and the iOS e-mail will have some further instructions on how to register the device. This is so the UDID is collected easily, and by letting the user follow these instructions, the device ID is automatically coupled to their account. To inform the user on the process, there is a note at the bottom of the e-mail. The only thing that remains now is for you to include the ID in the provisioning profile and create a new build. Only then will this user be able to install the app.

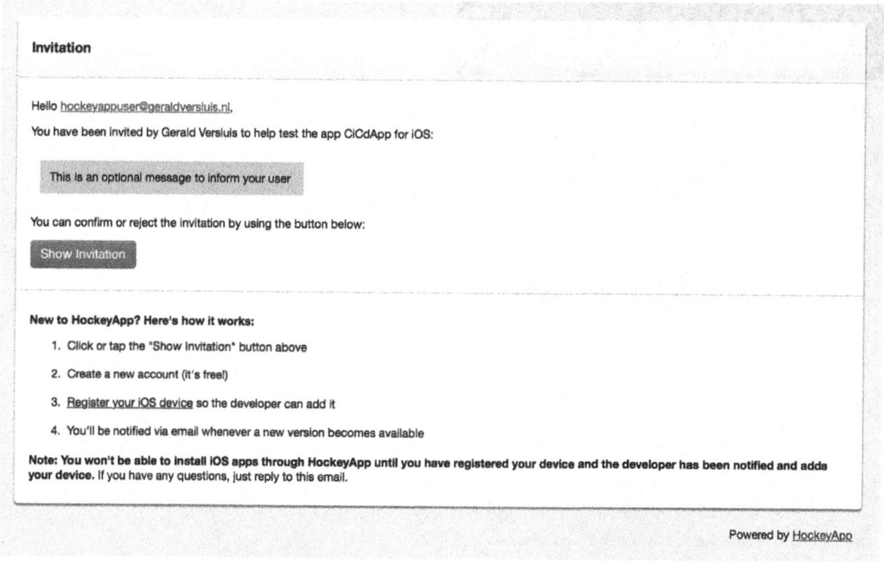

Figure 9-2. *The e-mail the user receives after being invited*

In the shaded box near the top the user will find the custom message you have provided, if you have provided one.

When users click the Show Invitation button, they are taken to the login page of HockeyApp. If they already have a HockeyApp account, they can log in with that. When they do, their account will be associated with your app, and they will be able to use it from within the account they already had. The other option is that they have to register for a new account. The result will be the same.

Let's take a look at what the user gets to see when you collect the device ID. Once again, there are multiple ways to get there. The user can either click the link at the bottom of the e-mail or navigate to the URL. The URL is `https://rink.hockeyapp.net/` and should be reached through the iOS device and with the Safari browser. Any other browser will *not* work. This is because of the way the ID is collected, which can be done only by installing a configuration profile on the iOS device. While this may sound quite heavy, in reality it really is not that bad. The only thing the profile can do is collect the ID and nothing more. Because other configuration profiles can have a lot more features, Apple has restricted installing these profiles solely through Safari.

When users navigate to the URL, they will be presented with a screen that provides them with instructions on how to proceed and what to expect. Figure 9-3 shows this screen.

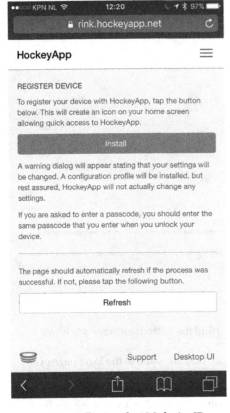

Figure 9-3. Collecting the iOS device ID

After clicking the Install button, the user will be taken to the iOS Settings app and the actual profile. This is where the user must decide to go through with it or not. If they want their ID to be collected automatically, they would be required to install the profile. Some details about the profile are listed, such as who the issuer is and what it does. The user can click into the details to learn more before installing it.

Figure 9-4 shows the screen to install the profile. The user can click either Install or Cancel.

■ **Tip** If users are not comfortable with installing the profile, then there is the possibility of supplying the UDID manually. The web site http://whatsmyudid.com/ provides an example way of finding the UDID with iTunes. You could give this URL to the user and have them report the ID themselves.

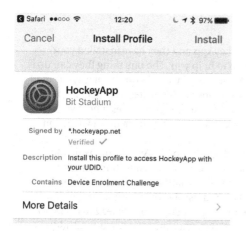

Figure 9-4. *Reviewing the profile and installing it on the device*

After the user has chosen to install the profile, they will be taken back to Safari, and their device details will be visible. If they were signed in at the time, the details (and thus device ID) are linked to their account. If they were not signed in, the details will be linked after signing in at that point.

This process is similar for Android and Windows, but those platforms do not need any special collection of device IDs. The details about the devices being used are still collected, so you can still see what device or devices are being used by users. If a user wants to add another device to their account, just have them go to the install URL again and log in to associate the device with them.

Another good thing to know is that you do not need to invite users via their HockeyApp account e-mail. If it turns out they already have an account, they can accept the invitation and log in with their existing account; the app will be associated with that account instead.

The only thing that remains is for the user to being able to see the apps they have access to and install them. For iOS, an icon was put on the home screen when the profile was installed. This is nothing more than a shortcut to the HockeyApp portal, which can also be reached manually by going to `https://rink.hockeyapp.net`. This should again be done from Safari, because only Safari can install apps from the browser. For UWP, you can also download the app straight from the web portal or even the notification e-mail received when a new version is available. For Android, an app is available in the Google Play Store to access the portal, but you can also access it through the Web.

> ■ **Note** When you receive errors while installing an app on iOS saying that the app cannot be downloaded at that time, make sure the device ID is in the provisioning profile. That is the main reason for errors in my experience. You can inspect which devices are currently in the provisioning profile of a specific version by going to the HockeyApp dashboard of that version and finding the Provisioning heading. There you can click through to an overview of all the associated devices.

Collecting Feedback

Now that you have seen how users look at HockeyApp and they have installed your apps, you can start looking at what they can do to help you. The one thing they can do is provide you with feedback. Of course, this can be done in a wide variety of ways: e-mail, social media, face to face. But to be as efficient as possible, it is best to collect feedback in a unified way. HockeyApp provides you with this. And not only does it help you with collecting the feedback, it also integrates with VSTS and can create a ticket when you receive feedback.

There are two ways of receiving feedback through HockeyApp: from inside the HockeyApp portal and by e-mail. When enabling the feedback collection, an e-mail address is created for you. When a message is received at that e-mail address, it will be reported as feedback to this particular app. The address, however, is not one you can easily remember. It will look something like this: support+49379723qwe1230b733a6c1 eac28@feedback.hockeyapp.net. To get around this, you can create an e-mail address yourself, like feedback@myapp.com, and set up a forward on it to the HockeyApp address.

The collection of feedback is something that is to be configured per app. To enable it, go into the app dashboard and click the Manage App button, as shown in Figure 9-5.

Figure 9-5. *Configuring the app settings*

In the settings, there is a section about the feedback, where you will notice that collecting feedback is enabled by default. This is where you can find the e-mail address that is set up for you. If you choose to disable the feedback collection, you can configure an e-mail address to be used as the reply-to address for invitation e-mails and update notification e-mails. This way, when a user sends feedback directly to one of those e-mails, it will not be lost. Just remember that with the feedback collection disabled, the user will not be able to provide feedback through HockeyApp directly.

Lastly, when you have feedback either enabled or disabled, you can configure a link to an external support system. If you use some other system to collect user feedback, enter the URL here, and it will be shown to the user in the feedback section.

When feedback collection is enabled, people can log into the HockeyApp portal and switch to the feedback section. This is shown in Figure 9-6.

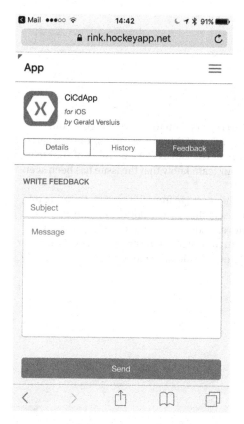

Figure 9-6. *Collecting feedback from the HockeyApp portal*

When a user fills out this form or sends an e-mail to the configured address, you will receive a new feedback item in your dashboard along with a notification in your e-mail inbox.

On the Feedback tab of your app, you will now see a new entry. All feedback entries are treated as conversations. In the overview, you will have all feedback items that are entered by users, as shown in Figure 9-7. Here you can see who submitted the feedback, when they submitted it, how many messages are in the conversation, and what the status is. Right from the overview you can change the status of the conversation.

Figure 9-7. *The feedback overview*

You can also click an item and go into the conversation to see what is going on.

When inside a conversation, there are a number of things you can do. You can set the status, just like from the overview, but in addition, you can assign a member of your team to this item. This way, you can let the rest of your team know that the issue has been seen and is being worked on.

Furthermore, you can add a response to the message from this screen. By doing this, the user is notified, and if ỹour message requires it, they can respond. This can be a way to engage your users and try to clear up whatever issue they might have. Another thing that can make your users happy is to keep them informed on the progress. That is another thing you can do from right here. Figure 9-8 shows the detail screen.

Figure 9-8. *Details of a feedback entry*

Not only messages from users will be shown in the discussion, but it also acts as a timeline. Whenever the status of the ticket changes, this will be reflected by a message in this discussion view.

If you have configured a bug tracking system to be attached to this app and enabled the creation of tickets, a ticket should appear in your bug tracking system. Depending on the bug tracking system, the synchronization will be both ways. For instance, when you change the status in the HockeyApp portal or in VSTS, it will be updated in the other system as well.

■ **Tip**   For a more integrated experience, you can also add in-app feedback. The
HockeyApp SDK provides you with a way to add the feedback collection right in your app
so the user does not have to leave the app to send you a message. To read more about this,
refer to https://support.hockeyapp.net/kb/client-integration-cross-platform/
how-to-integrate-hockeyapp-with-xamarin#feedback.

Basic Error Reporting

Besides letting the users provide their own feedback, there are also some ways to send
feedback from the app with more technical details. In most cases, this can be many times
more helpful than what the user reports. A lot of users will just write, "The app does not
work; I click *x* and it crashes, while I expect it do to *y*." But sometimes they don't even
provide you with that much detail. They are not to blame; most of the time they are not
technical people, and they do not know any better. However, this is too little information
to solve their problem. Also, when the user comes to you with bugs, most of the time you
are too late already. Especially while building apps, users are very critical. If it crashes
once, it can be forgiven, but when it happens again, your app is soon deleted, and it will
be hard to persuade the user to come back. Most of the time when a user does report
a bug, you are already too late. The majority of people will not bother to send you any
feedback and just delete the app.

Therefore, it can be helpful to detect errors even before the users do. Of course,
most of the errors should be filtered out with automated builds, unit tests, and UI tests,
but not everything can be detected that way. Because of this, it is important to have error
reporting in place. HockeyApp provides this for you in an easy-to-use way.

By default, when installing the SDK, error reporting is enabled. This means that
when an unhandled exception occurs, it is saved to the file system and sent back to your
HockeyApp account the next time the app is started. To account for the user's privacy,
HockeyApp has already built in a prompt to inform the user about what is happening.
This prompt, shown in Figure 9-9, asks the user if the report can be sent back to the
developer. They can also choose to allow it always.

Figure 9-9. *Allowing the app to send a report*

In Chapter 7 you saw how to integrate the SDK in your apps, and there is nothing extra you have to do to get this running. However, this functionality should be your last resort. While it is great to get a report of an unhandled exception, because it means an error has been identified that you did not spot earlier and you can fix it, ideally you want to catch all the exceptions and handle them gracefully.

An unhandled exception in the app ecosystem means the app will terminate without notice, and the user will be surprised for a second, requiring them to restart the app and enter any data they did before. To do it right, you want to catch the exception, notify the user something went wrong and how they can recover (if they can at all), and move along.

If you have been developing apps with Xamarin and used the HockeyApp predecessor, Xamarin Insights, you might know that you can report handled exceptions. Unfortunately, at the time of this writing, HockeyApp does not support that kind of functionality. There have been some messages on the support forum stating that this functionality will come, but no time frame has been given.

Tracking Custom Events

Besides getting crash reports, you might want to track a user's behavior throughout a session in your app. This can help you gain useful insights on how users are actually using your app, rather than thinking you know how they use your app.

This functionality can be useful to figure out all sorts of things: how many users defeat a level in your game, how often is an in-app purchase transaction started, was the purchase actually made, and how long a certain request takes. These are things that you could track.

The service to track all this was available in Xamarin Insights, and you could even identify users and sessions and follow them every step of the way. The implementation of this in HockeyApp is not quite there yet. You will get aggregated data of the events, but you will not be able to drill down into it and see all the details.

As I mentioned earlier, the responsibility of not collecting privacy sensitive data lies with you. This is probably the most important functionality to be careful with. As you will see in a little bit, it is easy to supply custom data with events. It can be convenient to collect some user-specific data to help you identify a problem or contact a user for more information. Although this can be tempting, be cautious about it. At least inform your users if you are doing so and, better yet, provide them a way to opt out.

The custom event tracking is part of the user metrics functionality of HockeyApp (which is what you will look at next), and thus enabling or disabling this will affect both the event tracking *and* collecting user metrics. For iOS, the functionality is enabled by default. If you want to disable it, you can do so with the following code in your AppDelegate.cs file:

```
// add the HockeyApp namespace
using HockeyApp.iOS;

// in your FinishedLaunching-method add:
var manager = BITHockeyManager.SharedHockeyManager;
manager.Configure("$Your_App_Id");
manager.DisableMetricsManager = true;
manager.StartManager();
```

It is important that you set the `DisableMetricsManager` property before you start the manager.

For Android, it is the exact opposite. It will be disabled by default, and you will have to enable it yourself. This functionality for Android is available only from API level 14 and up. To enable the custom events in Android, add this code in your `MainActivity.cs` file:

```
// add the HockeyApp namespace
using HockeyApp.Android.Metrics;

// in your main activity OnCreate-method add:
MetricsManager.Register(Application, "$Your_App_Id");
```

You can now start tracking your custom events. These events consist of a string identifier, which you can make up yourself. They should be self-describing, should be unique, and should have meaningful names. Make sure they do not look too similar and you know what they do when you read them. There are a few limits to this. The name is limited to lowercase and uppercase letters, numbers, underscores, dots, spaces, and hyphens.

■ **Note**   It is important to stick to the naming conventions. Not doing so will result in a silent failure and your event will simply not show up in the dashboard.

Also, there is a rate limit; you can send up to 350 unique event names per app, per week. However, one (unique) event has no limit on its occurrence. As a normal user, you should not hit that limit anytime soon, so you do not have to worry about that.

To create a new event, just make up the name and implement it in your code. The first time it occurs, it will start showing up in your dashboard. Before you start implementing an event, ask yourself what the main goal is. Maybe you want to identify a problem, you want to track performance, or you are interested in business goals. Decide on how you can measure the things you need and start implementing the gathering of information on it.

As I mentioned, it is your responsibility to not collect any sensitive data on your users.

To track an actual event, you can use the following code for iOS:

```
var manager = BITHockeyManager.SharedHockeyManager;
manager.MetricsManager.TrackEvent (eventName);
```

Or you can use this code for Android, which is quite similar:

```
HockeyApp.Metrics.MetricsManager.TrackEvent (eventName);
```

Some overloads are available that allow you to send additional data along with your custom event. This is done with key/value pairs in a dictionary. Here's an example of this for iOS:

```
manager.MetricsManager.TrackEvent(
"Sample_Event",
new NSDictionary { { "key", "value" } },
new NSDictionary { { "ExecutionTime", 1.0 } });
```

The first dictionary contains values that you want to supply for reference. In the second dictionary, you can add measurement data. It does not really matter what data you put in which dictionary, but if you use this code, the measurement data will be shown nicely.

When this event is now triggered from the app, it will show up in the HockeyApp dashboard, which is shown in Figure 9-10. Here you can see an overview of the last events that occurred. When you select one, the bottom half of the screen will reflect some more statistics about it. You can see how often the event was invoked, how many unique users it was invoked for, and what percentage of your total users that is.

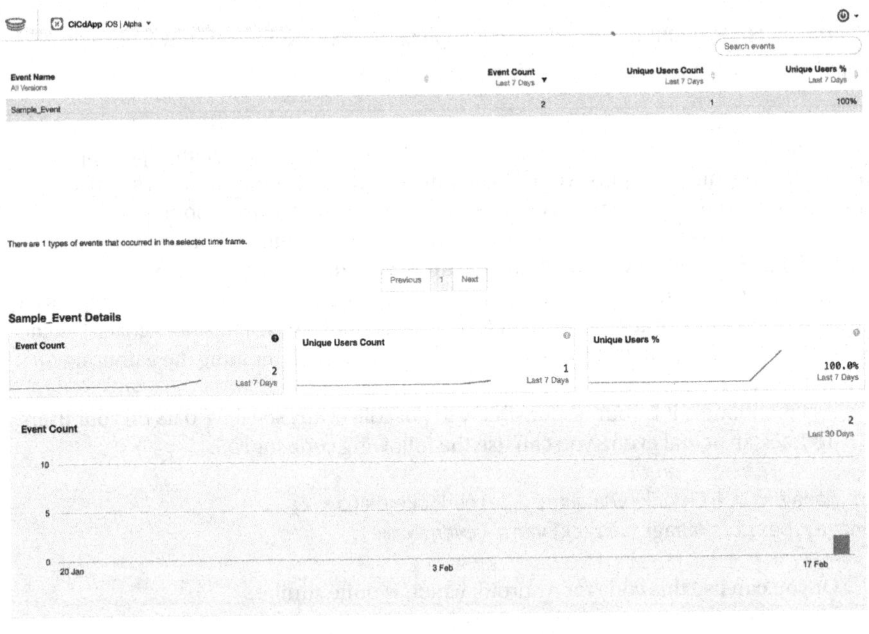

Figure 9-10. *Your custom events in the HockeyApp dashboard*

The thing that stands out is that the details you have supplied additionally are not available from the dashboard. At the time of this writing, this functionality is not available from within HockeyApp. It can, however, be accessed through Application Insights. Application Insights is very much like HockeyApp but more focused on web applications. It is available through Azure, and you will need to set up a bridge between the two. You can learn more about this at https://azure.microsoft.com/en-us/blog/access-hockeyapp-data-in-ai-with-hockeyapp-bridge-app/.

This concludes the topic of custom events. I hope this will be expanded more in the near future to make it even more valuable than it is now.

Analyzing Usage Statistics

From the HockeyApp dashboard of your app, you have direct access to some of the statistics that are available to you. These metrics are an overview of all the versions that you have in HockeyApp; however, you can filter them on a per-version basis. Figure 9-11 shows what these metrics look like.

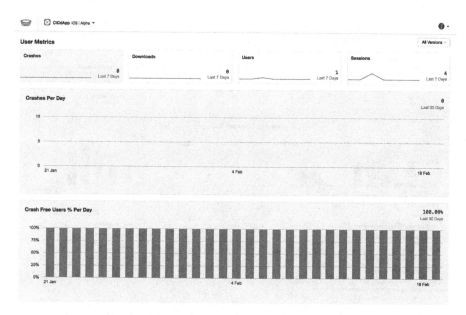

Figure 9-11. *Inspecting user metrics*

The graphs are mainly focused on how many crashes, downloads, users, and sessions there have been in the past week. With this data, you can quickly see whether your app is being used (and therefore tested) at all and how it is holding up. By clicking one of the four graphs at the top, you get some drill-down data on the screen. When clicking downloads, for example, you will be provided with a graph showing you the number of downloads per day.

If you use HockeyApp as a closed system for your testers and developers, you probably have less interest in these statistics. But when your app is available as an open test version, this is where you can see whether users are finding their way to it.

There is also some data available from within a crash report. Besides all the details that you can see about the crash, you can see how many users are impacted or how often the crash occurs per day.

With this data, you can make decisions on the priority of your bug. On projects I have worked on, these numbers became part of the service level agreements (SLAs). When a bug affected more than a certain percentage of users, there was no extra sign-off required; I just fixed it. It is also an awesome instrument to see whether regression on your work is happening. When you are convinced a bug is resolved, the numbers should go down over time. If they do not, you know something is still going wrong.

Finally, you can see what devices are affected. Maybe the problem only happens on these devices or maybe your user base just happens to use these devices the most, but in any case with these statistics you can gain some insight on this.

Figure 9-12 shows the numbers associated with a crash report; this image is provided by HockeyApp. (The numbers on my sample applications are too low to get the message across.)

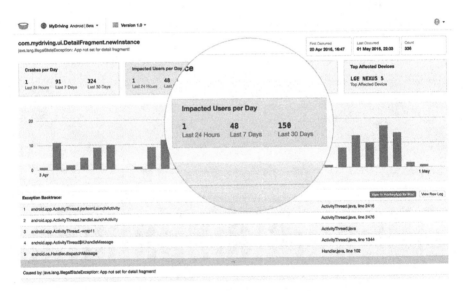

Figure 9-12. *User metrics in a crash report (image courtesy of HockeyApp)*

Throughout the HockeyApp dashboard there are some more places where charts and graphs are available to you. They all provide you with meaningful data in the given context. Per version there is also a Statistics section in the top bar.

In the Statistics section, you can see some facts about that specific version, such as which users have downloaded it, what devices they installed it on, and so on.

Update Distribution

One last thing you can do with the HockeyApp SDK is to update your distribution. In other words, you can notify users that an update is available. This works for either ad hoc or enterprise distribution as well as app store distribution. The only difference is that in the latter case you will only get a notification that an update is available. For ad hoc or enterprise distributed apps, you can also show the release notes of the new version right away and let the user download it from the alert directly.

This functionality is disabled by default. For me personally, I do not really like apps that notify me of new versions. That is what the app store is for, and if users want to update, it should be their choice. I can imagine that people would be annoyed that an alert is shown to them when they just want to quickly look up something in your app. Also, if you have a steady update cycle (because you have an automated pipeline now), this means you will alert your users maybe even every week. That is not desirable in my opinion. I could see some use for this in enterprise environments where you want to have more control over the version that your users are using, but then again the enterprise app store probably has some mechanism in place to force users to install an update.

If you want more information on this, see this documentation page: `https://support.hockeyapp.net/kb/client-integration-cross-platform/how-to-integrate-hockeyapp-with-xamarin#updated-distribution`.

Final Thoughts

In Chapter 7, you made your first acquaintance with HockeyApp; in this chapter, you looked a bit closer at what it can do for you. First, I showed you what HockeyApp looks like from a user's perspective. It can be helpful to know what the end users are seeing when they turn to you for help. You also saw how you can get to your app and install it onto a device.

Furthermore, you saw how user feedback is collected, again from the user perspective but also where it shows up in the HockeyApp portal for you to work with. Besides collecting feedback, you can also gather usage statistics and analyze them from the dashboard.

To learn more about the ways the user goes through your app, you can implement custom events. With these events, you can identify certain actions or measure how long operations take. This can be helpful to see what works for your audience or where you should improve loading times, for instance.

This chapter concludes the hands-on part of this book. In the next chapter, I will discuss how you can optimize the continuous integration and delivery pipeline even more. I will be giving you some ideas to think about when expanding your build definitions. Also, you will learn how the behavior of your developers is also important in all this, how you can get information to come to you instead of having to look for it, and how you go about using features that are not done yet.

CHAPTER 10

■ ■ ■

Where to Go from Here

Now that you have seen all that you can do, it is about time we part ways. But before we do, there is one more thing that I want to share with you. In this chapter, I will give you some ideas about where to go from here. What other things are there to incorporate in your pipeline, and how can you optimize your development process even more?

That is exactly what you will learn in this chapter. Each section will describe something that you can do to work more efficiently when using continuous integration and delivery with Xamarin apps.

Different Build Definitions

In Chapter 3 I mentioned that breaking up your build definitions into several definitions, each with its own purpose, is probably a good idea. The following are a couple of build definition variants that you can use. But remember to choose the ones that suit your requirements and do not implement any just because you feel it is a best practice. Also, this is not a complete list of different builds; it is intended merely to give you some ideas.

- *Continuous integration*: For a continuous integration build it is important that the time to complete the build is as short as possible. Therefore, try not to do too many tasks in a CI build definition. It is not necessary to version the assemblies or upload artifacts, as you will not use them. The CI build's main concern is to check whether the code still builds. In other words, you want to see whether code checked in by every member of your team still compiles. The only thing, besides building your code, that should be in the definition are unit tests. A continuous integration build will be triggered with each commit by a member of the team.

- *Nightly*: Nightly builds have been around for some time now. These builds are done every night (as the name might have given away) and typically *do* produce artifacts. Because the version could potentially be used and tested, you should increment the version number on it. If you are working with developers in different time zones, nightly might be an ambiguous term, so you will have to make some compromises. Because the build is triggered once every night and no one is actually waiting for its

© Gerald Versluis 2017
G. Versluis, *Xamarin Continuous Integration and Delivery*,
DOI 10.1007/978-1-4842-2716-9_10

results, a nightly build is a good build definition to enrich with some more automated tests. In this build, you can include the Xamarin Test Cloud tests, regression tests, and/or integration tests.

- *Canary*: The term *canary build* comes from the time when coal miners would take a canary with them to detect toxic gases in the mines. When the canary died, they would know that they had to get out of the mine. The same concept goes for canary builds, except no one dies. Ideally. With a canary build you push out new (maybe experimental) code to a subset of users. This can be a small percentage of the total users you have. This way, you can safely test some new functionality on them, without affecting the whole group. This build definition is a regular build that increments your version number and generates artifacts, but it is probably triggered by a specific branch that has the canary code.

- *Feature*: You can also create a build per feature. You might decide not to include feature branches in your CI builds because they will affect only a small number of people or maybe just one person at all, but you want to let someone know that their build is failing. To do this, you can create a definition just for feature branches. With the filter capabilities of VSTS that were described in Chapter 4, this should be easy to do. As for the tasks in these definitions, they are probably identical to the ones in a CI build because you want to know the results of the build as soon as possible.

- *Per platform*: To keep your builds fast and the feedback as on target as possible, you probably want to create a separate definition per platform. If you commit code to the iOS app, the results of a build of the Android app are not important to you at that time. Of course, when you are building Xamarin apps, this can get mixed up rather quickly because when you commit code to the shared portion of both apps, you *do* want to have them build both. This is something you can do with the filters explained in Chapter 4. With the folder filters, you can trigger a build depending on which folder code is committed. Setting this up correctly may take some thought, but when done right, it can be powerful.

- *Distribution*: Lastly, you can have a build that is linked directly to a release definition. This build will do everything it needs to deliver releasable artifacts, swap tokens, increment version numbers, and so on. Finally, the artifacts are uploaded, and a release will be triggered. Depending on what your other builds look like, you might want to do the last, full-blown test run on this to make sure everything is all right. This build could be linked to a commit on the master branch, so only when a merge happens from developer to master will you be presented with a new increment of your product.

I hope these different build definitions will give you some ideas on how to design your automated pipeline even better. Ideally, it should be a mix of different definitions to ensure the quality of your product from end to end. And you are the only one who knows how to do that best, so go try it for yourself! Just remember nothing is written in stone, so try something that you think will work, and if it doesn't work out as you would have hoped, fine-tune it until it does.

Expanding Your Build Definitions

You can expand your build definitions in a lot of ways. Up until now you have simply added tasks to build your code, increment the version number, and trigger tests on Test Cloud. Something that is not uncommon is the usage of tokens or API keys. These keys might differ depending on the environment you are connecting to; think of a Bing Maps token, for instance. Or, even more common is the URL you are connecting to in order to reach the back end of your application. You surely want to change that address between your development and production environments. This is something that can be done with automated builds, of course.

■ **Tip** One way to make values such as URLs more dynamic is to use configuration files. Since Xamarin does not have `app.config` files like other .NET applications, you should provide your own mechanism. A great one is provided by Adam Pedley in this blog post: `https://xamarinhelp.com/configuration-files-xamarin-forms/`. After implementing this configuration, you can replace the values with custom tasks called *tokenization tasks*. They just replace one token with another.

Another thing you might want to consider is checking the quality of your code while building. I discussed using SonarQube in Chapter 4. With this in place you can measure all kinds of cool stuff about your code. Another alternative or addition to this could be incorporating ReSharper. With ReSharper you can see whether your coding standards have been breached. Also, you can get some recommendations about where your code can be optimized. If you do not know ReSharper, there is also a plug-in for Visual Studio that is worth looking at. In addition, someone has made the power of ReSharper available in VSTS through the marketplace.

Whenever you think, "This is something I change or switch manually when releasing," you should see whether you can find a way to automate it through VSTS. Just try to take it one step at a time and gradually expand all your definitions with meaningful tasks.

The VSTS marketplace is a good place to browse and get some inspiration. Just see what is out there and think about whether and how you can put something to use for your own projects. Tasks are added every day, so by the time this book is in your hands, there should be a lot to choose from.

Feature Flags

A question that is much heard when implementing continuous delivery is, "What if a feature is so big that it cannot be completed before a deployment/delivery is done?" This is a valid question, and some features are bigger than others, but most will probably take up some time. Depending on your situation, the next deployment or delivery might be only a couple of hours away, so even if your feature is not that big, you might find yourself lacking time.

To overcome this challenge, you can use *feature flags* (also referred to as *feature toggles*). This concept describes a method where you "hide" certain features until they are complete. Only then you flip a switch—called a *flag*—so the functionality for that feature is available to the user.

The implementation of this can vary. There are even some frameworks to help you with the concept of feature flags, but in the simplest form it can be a Boolean that you evaluate to see whether a piece of code is in effect. In addition, you can flip those Booleans. The easiest way to do this is to set the value of your Boolean for a specific feature to true in your code and push that to the repository. A more advanced scenario would be to have the values of the feature flags in a configuration file so you can change their states on the fly. Even beyond that there is the possibility of administering a value remotely.

Depending on your requirements and situation, you can choose to implement different forms of this. As a single developer, you probably will not need to use this advanced functionality, but as your project and team start to grow, you will want to start looking into feature flags.

■ **Tip**   The Launch Darkly service provides you with the tools needed to get started using feature flags. It is easy to incorporate and has cool features to not only flip switches but also roll out feature flags to a certain percentage of users. This service is not free; it starts at $79 a month. For more information on this service, you can go to https://launchdarkly.com/.

For more information, as well as some warnings on how (not) to use feature flags, take a look at this article written by Martin Fowler: https://martinfowler.com/articles/feature-toggles.html.

Receiving Alerts

A lot of power of a continuous integration pipeline comes from the short feedback cycles, as you saw in Chapter 1.

Microsoft has built in a powerful alerting mechanism in VSTS, making it possible to receive alerts about almost anything. To get started with it, find the Notifications section in your VSTS dashboard, as shown in Figure 10-1.

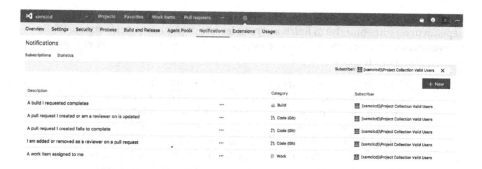

Figure 10-1. *Notifications overview in VSTS*

Here you can configure all kinds of alerts—not only alerts that have to do with builds succeeding or failing but also work items assigned to you. With this functionality, you can be sure that you will be informed about everything each step of the way. Whenever a trigger that you have defined here is invoked, you will get an e-mail message in your inbox right away.

■ **Tip** At the time of writing this book, there is a functionality called Out of the Box notifications that is available in preview. With it, you can set up notifications for everyone in your VSTS account with one click, or you can let them do it themselves. When you enable it, everyone will be provided with meaningful notifications. These notifications include but are not limited to feedback on a build that you have triggered, notices when you are requested for a code review, and notifications on the status of a pull request.

Without this out-of-the-box functionality you need to set up each notification manually. By the time you are reading this book, this might have been enabled by default. Regardless, you can still configure custom notifications with Out of the Box.

The Human Factor

This book focuses mainly on the tools and techniques that are available to you to establish a powerful and comprehensive automated build pipeline. But like most IT systems, the weakest links are the humans involved in the process. This section will focus on that.

To make sure that the quality of your product remains the best it can, you can use a whole lot of tools to support you. These tools are there when you are developing, when you have committed your code, and when a binary has been released. In this book, you have looked at some of them, and they can help you make the most out of it. Yet, it is still you—the developer—who must do the heavy-duty work. As your team starts to grow, the effort to make everything go smoothly will grow with it. Suddenly you find yourself dependent on someone else to finish a certain feature or produce a new version. While everyone is undoubtedly doing the best they can, it will help to create a few ground rules when working in a team.

- *Check-in early, check-in often*: If you want to make life easier on yourself, check in your code more often than not. This will prevent painful merge processes, and with the CI builds in place, you will get confirmation each time that your code still plays well with code checked in by others. This means checking in your code multiple times a day, and if by itself it does nothing, hide it with a feature flag. I would even go as far as to say that if your code is not checked in, it does not exist. Other people cannot anticipate code that is not there for them to see, so make sure it is there and it builds. Of course, wherever I say check in, you should read commit in terms of Git.

- *Do not check in any code that does not build*: All code that you commit should build. This may sound trivial, but saying it out loud makes it happen and makes people feel more responsible. To enforce this rule, you can use some features of Git such as pull requests and branch policies. I will talk about those later this chapter.

- *Do not check-in code after a build breaks*: To prevent one disaster from happening after another, do not attempt to save your code after someone else has broken the build. Not only does it make it worse when you do, but with this rule you also create a necessity to fix the build as soon as possible. By setting this rule you effectively say when the build is broken, everyone will stall in their work. This way, the person responsible for breaking the build will feel more obligated to fix it and fix it fast. And of course, they will be more cautious next time.

- *No code without tests*: Everyone is convinced that you should have unit tests, but actually creating them and keeping them current is something that doesn't always happen. By coming up with a rule that no code is checked in without accompanying tests, you obligate everyone to do so. This way all code has at least one test, and thus the code quality should go up.

- *No commits after 4 p.m.*: It is a natural thing to check in your code right before you go home for the day, especially when you're going on vacation the next day. But the next day when your colleagues discover that the code you have committed does not work as intended or does not even build at all, they have two choices: either ignore it and wait for you to come back or—what is most likely to happen—fix it for you because they cannot wait for you to come back.

That is not a responsibility that you want to delegate to your colleagues. If you have code that is nearing completion at the end of the day, it is nothing that cannot wait until tomorrow to be merged into the branch. Make sure you check in your code at a time when you can verify the results.

- *Every commit should be able to go to production*: Every time that you commit code, just think to yourself, "What would happen if this code goes to production?" By doing so, you will make sure that the code you produce will not behave badly in the hands of the customer. So, either the code works perfectly or you should consider hiding it with a feature flag or some other feature.

Like I stated earlier, most of these rules are based on a commitment made by you and your team members. This, however, does not mean you cannot use some tools or other means to accomplish them.

One way to do this is to implement code reviews. Before any code is checked in definitively, you could ask someone to review the code that you have produced. The code should be ready to merge with the rest of the code and thus include all tests, and so on. One or more team members will take a look at your code and provide you with some constructive feedback. Whenever everyone is happy with the result, the code can be merged.

A great way to do this when you are using Git is by using *pull requests*. A pull request is basically an inquiry to another member of your team to allow your code to be pulled into the main branch. This way, you make sure that at least one person has had the opportunity to look at your code before it becomes part of the repository.

But you can take it even further than that. With the latest features regarding Git in VSTS, you can implement *branch policies*. This is a powerful feature that can give you fine-grained control over what code is merged into a branch, and by whom.

It also takes some work out of your hands. For instance, one of the configuration options lets you trigger a build definition whenever a pull request is done. So, when someone sends a pull request to a branch, a build of your choosing is triggered, and you will know whether it integrates or not. On top of that, you can demand that the build that is triggered is no older than a specific number of hours. If the build passes that limit and the pull request is not merged, a new build should be requested and pass before the pull request can be merged at all. By doing this, you are making sure that the code in the pull request is still compatible with the code that has been merged in the meantime.

There are a lot of other options that you can configure to do this, and they will only grow in the feature. Figure 10-2 shows the configuration screen for a branch policy.

Figure 10-2. *Configuring a branch policy*

Combined with the rights management you can set on the repository, you can set who has power over the master branch. Imagine a scenario where you put all your lead developers and/or architects in a separate group and give them rights to perform merges on the master branch. Then you implement a branch policy like the one shown earlier, and suddenly there is no way past the lead developer or architect to get code to production anymore. This effectively means that at least one trained, experienced pair of eyes has looked at it.

The last option that I want to point out to you is at the very bottom of the screen. You can configure paths within your repository to which you can assign specific reviewers. When you have your back-end code and your app code in one repository, you can assign someone from the mobile team and the API team who will be requested to take a look whenever code is committed to that specific portion of the repository.

Final Thoughts

I hope you have enjoyed reading this book as much as I have enjoyed writing it. I know it is a cliché to say, but it is a cliché for a reason. This is the first book I have written, and I have learned a lot from it while enjoying the process at the same time. I hope that I have been able to teach you a thing or two as well.

With this book I sought to provide you with everything you need to get a head start on using Xamarin continuous integration and delivery. Not every product feature is etched out in stone yet, and I am sure that by the time this book hits the stores there will be more power available to you than what I have described here. That is why I have focused not only on technique but also on some concepts that have to do with continuous integration and delivery. This way, you will know what is out there in the world to optimize your software development process, and let's be honest, this will save you from a lot of the frustration that comes from doing repetitive jobs such as releasing software.

If you can't figure something out, want some advice, or just want to tell me your thoughts about this book or anything in it, please do not hesitate to find me and reach out. You can do so on Twitter by my handle @jfversluis or e-mail me on gerald@verslu.is.

APPENDIX

■ ■ ■

Alternative Tooling

In this book, I have focused on Microsoft technologies, mainly because I love the Microsoft technology stack. The tooling is great, the languages are evolving beautifully, and in the past few years Microsoft has taken giant steps toward working with the community and putting effort into going open source. Because Microsoft is a big company, it also has a lot of capacity to push out great products at a steady pace. There are a variety of products, and they all work together well, so unless you really want to, you do not have to leave the .NET ecosystem for anything.

However, being a good developer means you must know what is out there. Do not create a blind spot by focusing on just one vendor and what it tells you. Remain critical, ask questions, and seek alternatives. Before and while writing this book, that is exactly what I did. Therefore, this appendix will show you that there are other products available. All the products and services I will teach you about in this appendix have their own strengths and weaknesses—some of them technically, others in licensing or pricing.

I will not go over the specifics of each alternative in this chapter. I will show you that there are other paths to take, and depending on the requirements you might have or the situation you are in, you can make an informed decision on what to use.

Most of the services I will describe like to play with others, and they have APIs you can use or they can make use of the APIs of others. This way you are not stuck in one ecosystem; you can cherry-pick the products and services you like and tie them together to create your own optimized pipeline.

Despite wanting to provide you with alternatives, there is one player that comes from Microsoft that I cannot ignore, so I will start off with one more Microsoft product.

Visual Studio Mobile Center

With the acquisitions of Xamarin and HockeyApp, Microsoft had some overlap in technologies in its portfolio. Xamarin Insights and the reporting capabilities of HockeyApp are quite similar yet not exactly the same. In addition, Microsoft has been busy developing solutions on top of Azure such as Application Insights.

To unify all the features and rebrand Xamarin Insights and HockeyApp in the process, Microsoft has announced the Visual Studio Mobile Center. While it is still in preview at the time of this writing, Visual Studio Mobile Center looks promising. It will be the replacement for Test Cloud, HockeyApp, and Insights, as well as part of VSTS.

© Gerald Versluis 2017
G. Versluis, *Xamarin Continuous Integration and Delivery*,
DOI 10.1007/978-1-4842-2716-9_11

With Mobile Center, Microsoft is creating a service that offers everything regarding mobile and everything I have talked about in this book. Microsoft is taking all the key features from the products it has now and putting them into one good-looking service. With Mobile Center, you can connect to your VSTS, GitHub or Bitbucket repository, get your Objective-C/Swift, React Native, or Xamarin app, and build it. When you have a build setup, you can automatically let it flow over to distribution and send it to your users.

Figure 11-1 shows the dashboard of a test app I have put in Mobile Center.

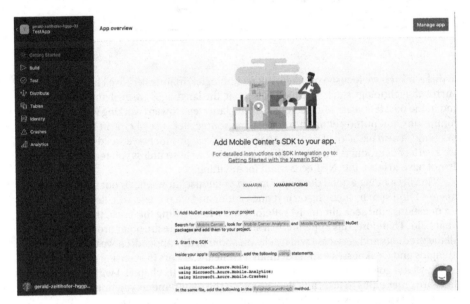

Figure 11-1. *Getting started page for my test app in Visual Studio Mobile Center*

Microsoft has introduced a whole new set of NuGet packages that you can integrate easily, which allows you to receive crash reports and analytics, just like you would with HockeyApp or Xamarin Insights. To complete the cycle, Microsoft has integrated the Test Cloud runs and results in Mobile Center. Finally, when you link your Azure subscription, you can easily integrate data storage and identity into your app without breaking a sweat.

All this goodness has been poured into a sleek-looking single-page application, with instructions to get you started every step of the way.

Now, I can almost hear you thinking, "Why shouldn't I use this over everything you have described in this book?" That is a valid question.

I have been informed by the Microsoft team that the Mobile Center will be the coming together of the Xamarin, HockeyApp, and some Azure services that have to do with mobile. However, it is not meant to be a replacement for all the functionality in VSTS. If anything, it is a springboard to the full-featured VSTS environment. Under the hood, Mobile Center leverages the build and release engine that is also being used in VSTS and TFS. Most likely, this will be positioned as a starting point for beginner developers or developers with simple requirements, offering them with an easy-to-use service for building their apps.

In the future, there might even be a migration path from Mobile Center to VSTS, where all of your build definitions (which are not called as such in Mobile Center) are already available to you as you have designed them from within Mobile Center.

Also, there is a great future ahead for Mobile Center, but we are not there yet. During this transition HockeyApp and Test Cloud will still be supported, even for a while after Microsoft announces the discontinuation of these services.

Even if you choose to get started with Mobile Center, what you have learned in this book will help you grasp the concepts behind it, and you will have a head start when transitioning to the much more advanced Visual Studio Team Services.

Once again, at the time of this writing, Mobile Center has just been introduced and is still in preview, as it will probably be for some time to come. Because of this, no pricing information is available at this time. Like with most Microsoft products, you can use it for free while it's in preview, but when the preview phase comes to an end, there probably will be costs, at least for parts of the functionality.

Finally, Mobile Center has one big advantage over VSTS: Mobile Center has provisioned the Mac hardware for you, so you do not need to do anything extra to build your iOS apps.

■ **Tip**　Want to know what is upcoming with Mobile Center? You can check out the road map at https://docs.microsoft.com/en-us/mobile-center/general/roadmap.

Bitrise

Bitrise (https://bitrise.io) is an all-in-one solution for building your app. It offers you basically the same functionality as VSTS does with its build definitions. However, it offers you the Mac hardware, so you do not have to worry about that part yourself.

The service is completely free to some extent. If you are able to get by with 2 users, builds that do not take longer than 10 minutes, and no more than 200 builds a month, you have nothing to worry about. You can have an unlimited number of apps and build definitions.

After that, prices start at $50 a month, as shown in Figure 11-2.

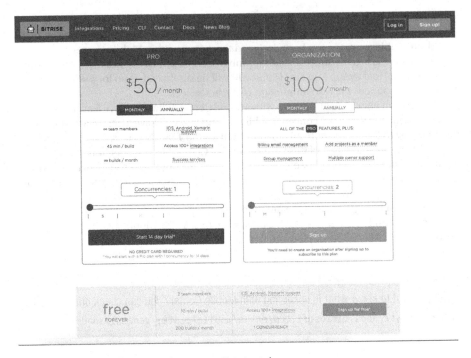

Figure 11-2. Pricing at Bitrise (courtesy of bitrise.io)

Apart from the naming, the features are largely the same as in VSTS. The build definitions are called *workflows* in Bitrise and have tasks in them. These tasks are all open source, and there is a repository available where you can get additional tasks. Because Bitrise has been around since 2014, it already has a stuffed library with all kinds of tasks that you can include in your workflow. These tasks range from useful ones, such as transferring your app to Test Cloud or HockeyApp, to some less useful ones, such as getting a random quote in your build log to keep you entertained while building is in progress. Figure 11-3 shows an example of a workflow.

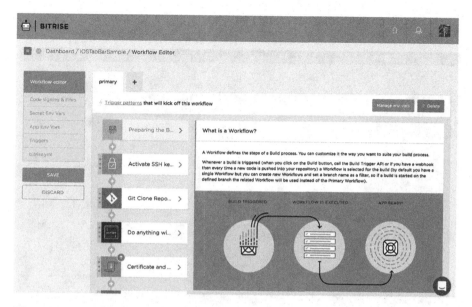

Figure 11-3. Workflow screen in Bitrise

Because of the free tier, great community that is behind it, and the provisioning of Mac hardware, Bitrise is a real treat. It is a great way to get started building your apps in an automated fashion, and it has the power to drive your big enterprise apps as well.

Besides building workflows that matter, you can integrate a whole lot of other services. Your code can come from any Git source, and builds can be triggered by a schedule, webhook, or manually. Learn more about the product at https://www.bitrise.io/integrations.

Since Bitrise is not focusing on Microsoft technologies and is not even running on Windows machines, building and running unit tests from MSTest are not supported. You can build Xamarin apps, as well as Java and Objective-C/Swift apps.

All in all, Bitrise is worth checking out.

AppVeyor

The final competitor in the automated build landscape I will introduce is AppVeyor (https://www.appveyor.com/). AppVeyor provides you with automated builds for .NET-based projects, but it does not have the user-friendliness in terms of compiling your own build definition on a workflow. Instead, you get a predefined workflow that you can configure in any way you like. If you want something more flexible, you will have to get your hands dirty with PowerShell and/or command-line commands. But if you do not want to do anything too advanced, the basic UI and functionality will get you there.

You can connect your repository from any popular service, including GitHub and VSTS. From there you can select the project that you want to build and start configuring it. The greatest thing about AppVeyor might be the pricing. For open source projects it is completely free!

For details on the pricing, see Figure 11-4.

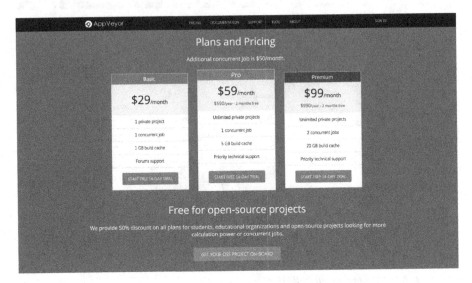

Figure 11-4. *Pricing on the AppVeyor service (courtesy of appveyor.com)*

Because you can use it for free, this service is perfect for automating any NuGet packages that you might have or, of course, any open source apps. I have been using AppVeyor in conjunction with GitHub to push out some of my NuGet packages.

Setting up AppVeyor is an easy thing to do: connect your GitHub account, choose the project, and configure it with your NuGet account to set up deployment. That's basically it!

When setting up AppVeyor from your GitHub repository, AppVeyor will install some webhooks for you. This way, whenever a pull request is received, it will automatically start a CI build for you and show the results right there, integrated in GitHub. To top it off, AppVeyor has badges, so you can show off the build status on any page anywhere with a badge. (By the way, this is also true for Bitrise and even VSTS.)

Figure 11-5 shows you how AppVeyor looks. On this screen, you can see the configuration of one of my NuGet packages.

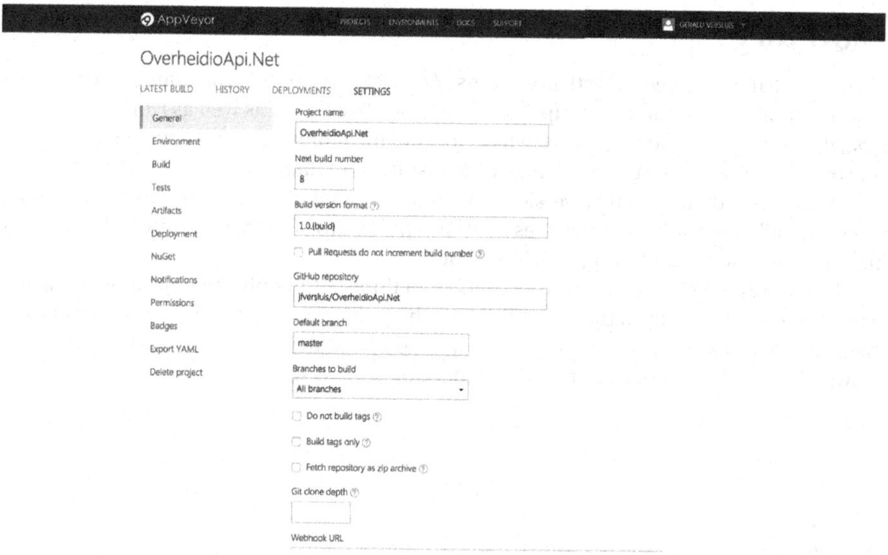

Figure 11-5. *Configuring an automated build with AppVeyor*

As you can see, there are a lot of possibilities already available to you. Besides creating builds, you can run tests, define artifacts and choose what to do with them, and deploy to one of the prebuilt deployment providers offered.

If you are working with NuGet and you do not want to push your package to the general NuGet feed for some reason, you can set up your own feed through AppVeyor.

Head over to the AppVeyor web site to see what it has to offer you.

Fastlane

Fastlane (`https://fastlane.tools/`) is bit of an odd one out. Let me say up front that I do not have any hands-on experience with it; however, it seems promising. With Fastlane, you compile a so-called fastfile, which describes a configuration that you want to use for your app. Right now, it supports only Apple and Android apps.

This fastfile can do a range of things, including incrementing your version number, distributing your app to HockeyApp or the App Store, signing your code, and much more. Working with it is not as obvious as all the other alternatives. On the Fastlane web site, you can compile a fastfile to start, but installation then has to be done on your project source files.

You import an installation script that you should run. From there on out you have a set of new commands at your disposal, all starting with the `fastlane` keyword.

Everything is open source on the GitHub page (`https://github.com/fastlane`), and there are also a great number of example repositories associated with the account. It seems promising in terms of saving you time; for example, it can automate creating screenshots in different screen sizes and localizations for you.

185

TestFairy

As the name might suggest, TestFairy (`https://testfairy.com/`) is an alternative to Test Cloud. Actually, it combines a couple of things from Test Cloud as well as HockeyApp. First, this is no automated test service like HockeyApp. It only provides you with a way to get your app to your testers easily and gather results from them.

It will help you distribute a version of your app to a set of testers, and from there you will get detailed reports on the test sessions. It is pretty awesome but requires a lot more human interaction than testing with Test Cloud.

From a test session, you can see a number of things. Probably the most interesting to see is a screen recording all the steps that a test has taken leading up to an error. Besides that, you get a whole lot of graphs and statistics about the device a tester is on. Figure 11-6 shows what a session looks like on a demo page on its web site.

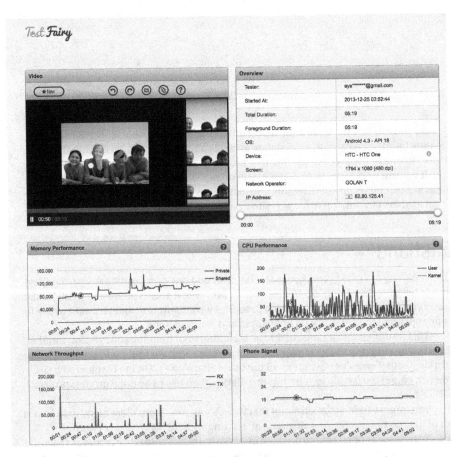

Figure 11-6. *TestFairy session on the demo account (courtesy of testfairy.com)*

Details about the device include but are not limited to CPU and memory usage, GPS, network, and more.

Because a session happens through an actual person on an actual device, you do have some more power and control over the device and scenarios than you have with Test Cloud. For instance, you can test on other networks than Wi-Fi, use Bluetooth, and so on.

Another cool feature is the report on test coverage. TestFairy can generate a report for you, with which you can see on one axis all the screens within your app (Activities/Fragments for Android and ViewControllers on iOS) and on the other axis all the devices. By creating a matrix like this, you can easily see how much ground is covered on each device and thus by each tester. Figure 11-7 shows an example of this matrix.

Figure 11-7. Test coverage per device (courtesy of TestFairy.com)

Furthermore, TestFairy has integrations with some popular issue-tracking tools such as Jira, Bugzilla, and even Trello, and from the portal you can easily create tickets in those systems. The integration works both ways and creates links to relevant information.

Basic distribution can be done without integrating the SDK into your app. However, if you want to gain more insights, you do need to incorporate it.

Pricing is free for the basic package, but there are paid tiers available for startups and enterprises. However, there are no prices listed on its web site at the time of writing.

Flurry

Flurry (https://developer.yahoo.com/) is a service from Yahoo. It offers several services with different names, targeting different functionality. I will be focusing on Flurry Analytics. This service is an alternative to HockeyApp and provides you with the same capabilities as HockeyApp and more.

By integrating the SDK, you immediately gain the ability to report events and crashes just like you would with HockeyApp. It will catch unhandled exceptions, but you can also manage exceptions that you handle in code so you can inspect them from the dashboard. Figure 11-8 shows a sample of this dashboard.

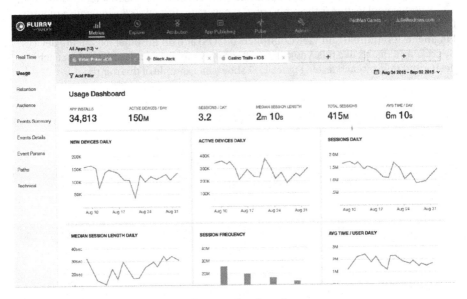

Figure 11-8. *The Flurry dashboard (courtesy by Flurry)*

Flurry also offers the ability to report events, so you can track a user's movement throughout your app.

It does not stop there. As you might have noticed, the graphs and data look similar to Google Analytics (which, by the way, can also be used in your apps), and it also has some Analytics-like data. You can see the demographic numbers of your audience, get information about active users or devices, and much more.

There is no notable integration to other services, other than their own.

Most of the data is available to you in real time, and with the service being free, it is worth trying.

■ **Note**   Flurry does not advertise Xamarin support on its web site. There are, however, some libraries available to help you integrate the SDK into your Xamarin app. Take a look at this repository to get you started: `https://github.com/mattleibow/Flurry.Analytics`.

Raygun

Another service that is about crash reporting and analytics is Raygun (https://raygun.com/), which is broken into two products: Crash Reporting and Pulse. The first one is obviously all about the crashes, and the latter is about finding and fixing performance issues.

Neither product has a free tier; pricing starts at $49 per month for the crash reports and $99 for Pulse. There is, however, a 14-day free trial available for you without the need of a credit card.

Raygun supports not only apps, but like Application Insights, it supports a great variety of programming languages and platforms. Integrating into a .NET project is as simple as just installing the right NuGet package and implementing a few lines of initialization code.

Raygun supports a great number of development platforms and has a big list of integrations to choose from. You can choose to get your source code from GitHub, VSTS, and more. You can track issues in Jira, Zendesk, VSTS, and more, and you can deploy your app through the integrations with Octopus Deploy, Powershell, FAKE, and more. Besides the integrations that are available to you out of the box, Raygun also offers webhooks and an API, like almost all the other solutions mentioned in this chapter.

All of this makes for a powerful and complete solution, but it comes at a price.

Figure 11-9 shows the dashboard. All the data is available in real time, and you can drill down through the data. If you have worked with Xamarin Insights before, you will be happy to look at Raygun because it has similar functionality to track users and their sessions throughout your application.

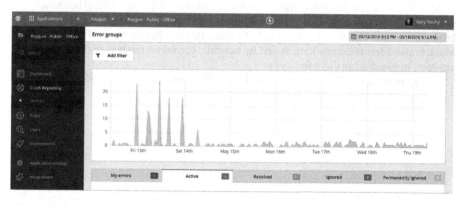

Figure 11-9. The Raygun dashboard (courtesy by Raygun)

Jenkins

As an alternative to VSTS, you can look at the Java-based Jenkins (https://jenkins.io/). Although I do not have extensive hands-on experience with Jenkins, I do know that it roughly offers the same functionality as VSTS, or at least TFS. It can take care of automated builds for you, as well as integrating code, delivering artifacts, and so on. Basically, it can do anything that has to do with building and releasing.

Jenkins has been around for a long time and is completely open source; it is available on GitHub. Managing the system goes through a web interface, although you will find that it is less user-friendly than VSTS.

Managing configurations and build tasks is done through so-called Jenkinsfiles, which are rather powerful but need some adjusting. As far as I know, there are no Jenkins-as-a-service providers around, so you will have to set it up yourself on a web server of your choosing.

Using Jenkins is free of charge and has a great community behind it; therefore, you can find a lot of support and up-to-date plug-ins for it. With the plug-in system in place, you can establish connections with services such as HockeyApp, Test Cloud, and all the other goodies you have learned about.

TeamCity

Just like Jenkins and VSTS, there is also TeamCity (https://www.jetbrains.com/teamcity/), which is a solution by JetBrains. Like Jenkins, TeamCity is built on Java and targets build management and continuous integration.

JetBrains does provision you with a hosted environment, which even has a free tier for up to 20 build configurations and 3 build agents. From there you can go to an enterprise license. For open source projects, you can request a free license, which gives you all the enterprise features as well.

TeamCity has some notable features such as gated commits, which you might already know about from VSTS. This means that no code gets checked in whenever a build is broken. It has extensive integrations with its own IDE (IntelliJ IDEA) but also Eclipse and even Visual Studio. Maybe the best feature is the built-in support for code inspections, coverage, and duplication. In Chapter 10, I briefly mentioned ReSharper, which is also a JetBrains product. TeamCity basically combines the best of these two products by integrating them for you.

You can use a variety of source control systems, including Git, CVS, TFS, and VSTS.

Figure 11-10 shows a typical TeamCity dashboard.

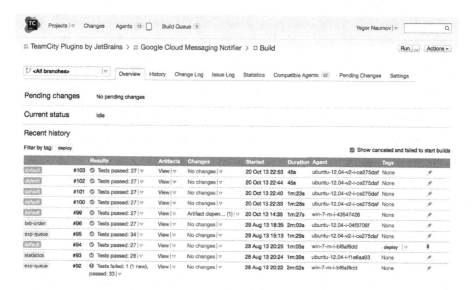

Figure 11-10. *TeamCity dashboard (courtesy by JetBrains)*

Final Thoughts

I hope you have learned a lot from this final chapter. I know I have. It can be powerful to see what other parties are doing and how you can benefit from that. You can combine different solutions and thus the strong points of each service to create the perfect environment for you.

If you put all of this into context with the Xamarin app development, it is safe to assume that Microsoft products are still the easiest to integrate with each other, because they all come from the same company. Still, you might come across other solutions that provide you with just a little bit extra. The little details can make your life easier while producing awesome apps.

If there is any service or product that I have missed, which there are plenty, please let me know because I am always interested to see what it is going on in other places. I am also interested in the ways that you have set up a pipeline for yourself and how my book has helped you do that.

Once more, thank you for reading.

Index

© Gerald Versluis 2017
G. Versluis, *Xamarin Continuous Integration and Delivery*,
DOI 10.1007/978-1-4842-2716-9

Get the eBook for only $5!

Why limit yourself?

With most of our titles available in both PDF and ePUB format, you can access your content wherever and however you wish—on your PC, phone, tablet, or reader.

Since you've purchased this print book, we are happy to offer you the eBook for just $5.

To learn more, go to http://www.apress.com/companion or contact support@apress.com.

Apress®

Printed in the United States
By Bookmasters